ISLAM
AND THE
BIBLE

ISLAM AND THE BIBLE

WHY TWO FAITHS COLLIDE

DAVID GOLDMANN

MOODY PUBLISHERS
CHICAGO

© 2004 by
DAVID GOLDMANN

Library of Congress Cataloging-in-Publication Data

Goldmann, David, 1931-
   Islam and the Bible : why two faiths collide / David Goldmann.
      p. cm.
   Includes bibliographical references.
   ISBN 0-8024-1017-0
      1. Islam—Relations—Christianity. 2. Christianity and other religions—Islam. 3. Islam—Doctrines. I. Title.

BP172.G635 2004
261.2'7—dc22
                                                        2003028136

3 5 7 9 10 8 6 4 2

In memory of
Dr. John W. Alexander,
president of InterVarsity
Christian Fellowship (1965–1981)
and a man of God used by our Lord as my mentor.
His godly modeling, wisdom,
and faithful prayer support have inspired me.

And

in appreciation to
Hamid, Ahmad, Muhammed, Mustapha
Omar, Abd Smed, Hassan, and Said
for great fellowship through the years
and their continued commitment to the
Lord Jesus Christ.

CONTENTS

FOREWORD

Just this week in Charlotte North Carolina, I had a taxi ride with a Muslim driver. I pointed out to him that in the Quran, Jesus is purported to have done greater miracles than Muhammad, and he agreed.

"Yes," he said, "Jesus did greater miracles than Muhammad; it's in our Quran." From there I was able to direct the conversation to reasons why this man should consider Jesus as the only one who is able to forgive our sins and represent us before God. We parted as friends, not antagonists; I can only pray that my witness led him a step closer to accept the Savior we love.

This is why I am so glad to endorse this book by my good friend David Goldmann. As someone who lived in North Africa for twenty-four years, David and his wife, Mary Lou, know the value of friendships in the Muslim community. Many years ago, I was able to observe firsthand their love of people, and their sincere desire to build bridges with their Muslim friends. Through their lives and witness

Muslims have come to know Christ, and other believers in these countries have strengthened to share their faith.

This book will not only help you understand Islam; it will also give you the knowledge you need to befriend the Muslims who are in your neighborhood. Whatever you might think of Islam as a religion, the fact is that there are thousands of people who are followers of Muhammad who will never know Jesus as Savior unless believers become their friends. Long ago I learned that we can never make Jesus attractive to Muslims if we antagonize them.

Here is a suggestion: Read this book with someone else; your spouse, your prayer partner, or even a casual friend who wants to learn more about the Muslim faith. Then interact with one another, discussing what you have learned and role playing with Muslim/Christian dialogue. I promise that you will benefit and actually look forward to the next opportunity of meeting a Muslim, whether in a taxi cab or in your home.

You are holding in your hands a book that will help you be a witness to the millions of Muslims God has brought to the United States and Canada; my prayer is that God will use this book widely to equip his people to be effective representatives of Jesus Christ in our diverse culture. We've spend millions of dollars and untold manpower to send people overseas to share the gospel with Muslims. Now that they are on our doorstep, God is calling each of us to be a loving witness to those whom we meet and befriend.

With this book you are embarking on an adventure that just might change your life and the lives of the Muslims we are privileged to reach with the good news.

PASTOR ERWIN LUTZER
MOODY CHURCH, CHICAGO.

ACKNOWLEDGMENTS

I'm thankful to Karen Oliver for editing and critiquing this book. Special thanks to Susie Pyatt for entering this material into the computer.

Both Dr. Greg Livingstone and Rev. Robert Blincoe reviewed the manuscript and gave many helpful suggestions. I am thankful to Jim Vincent, Mark Tobey, and the rest of the editorial staff at Moody Publishers, who were instrumental in the book's development.

I also profoundly thank my wife, Mary Lou, for her patience and perseverance during the writing of this book.

PREFACE

The Cross has been the symbol of Christianity for the past two thousand years. The wonderful purpose of God's anointed deliverer, Jesus Christ, was to die on the cross to free men and women from sin's oppression. Jesus demonstrated His power, even over death, through His resurrection.

Islam is a religion that offers an alternative to Christianity. It arose in the seventh century under the leadership of Muhammad. "Islam" means "submission to the will of Allah." A person who submits is a Muslim.

Today the Muslim world is no longer "somewhere else"; instead, North America has become part of the Muslim world. In the United States alone, four to six million Muslims are living in local neighborhoods, sharing workplaces and attending our schools and universities.

To understand the beliefs and practices of followers of Islam, we need to look at the beliefs and practices as found in Islam's holy books. Throughout *Islam and the Bible* I will quote from the translation of the Quran by Mohammed Pickthall in *The Meaning of the Glorious Koran;* all bracketed material are additions by Pickthall for clarification in his translation. I will also quote from the nine-volume Arabic-English collection of Al-Bukhari's *Hadith.*

Muslims desire to play an influential role in American life, culture, and politics. "The American Muslim Council, began in 1990, works to give Muslims a voice on issues of ethics and public policy," notes American church historian Timothy George. "Among other things, this group wants to counter the notion that American principles of morality and justice are based on the Judeo-Christian tradition alone. They favor the more inclusive idea of such values deriving from the Judeo-Christian-Muslim tradition."[1]

Muslim traditions regarding morality and justice, however, still vary from those of the Christian faith, as we will see in chapter 3. Among several differences, in Islamic law a woman is inferior to man, with lesser credibility as a witness and having a lesser share in any inheritance (Sura 2:282; 4:11). And while in the Judeo-Christian tradition it is not a crime to turn way from one's faith, anyone who forsakes Islam is considered an apostate, one who has renounced religious faith. According to Muhammad, the penalty is death (Hadith 9:57).

Despite these conflicts of morality and justice between the Judeo-Christian and Muslim traditions, Christians need to reach out with Christlike love and godly wisdom to the Muslim community. They need to befriend Muslims and present the good news of Jesus Christ.

This book will attempt to inform Christians about the Islamic religion, provide a better understanding of the uniqueness of the Christian faith, and offer ways to present the Gospel effectively to Muslims.

ONE

IS TRUE ISLAM PEACEFUL OR MILITANT?

The answer to this opening question is not simple, for there are many faces to Islam. Muslim clerics in the United States say that Islam means peace and doesn't sanction terrorist acts. Yet many clerics in other countries, such as Saudi Arabia, Iran, Pakistan, and Sudan, teach that committed Muslims must fight unbelievers (Jews and Christians) until they are subdued.

Muhammad, a prophet living in the seventh century, received revelations that he believed came from God, who identified Himself as Allah. Those revelations came to Muhammad to meet needs that arose on specific occasions. The revelations were gathered and recorded as the Quran (sometimes called the Koran), which has 114 chapters, or suras. Muhammad and those who followed him believed those revelations formed the Word of Allah.

Some revelations in the Quran are kind to non-Muslims.

Other revelations are adversarial. *Either position can be argued by quoting specific Quranic verses.*

Let's look at why Islam sometimes appears as a religion divided.

PEACEFUL *AND* MILITANT QURANIC REVELATIONS

During Muhammad's years in Mecca and early years in Medina, he made it easy for Jews and Christians to co-exist with Muslims. Adherents of Islam faced Jerusalem when praying, and Muhammad's message was tolerant toward Jews and Christians. Early passages in the Quran advocate a peaceful coexistence with Christianity.

> Lo! those who believe [in that which was revealed unto thee, Muhammad] and those who are Jews and Christians ... whoever believeth in Allah and the Last Day and doeth right—surely their reward is with their Lord. (Sura 2:62)

> There is no compulsion in religion. (Sura 2:256)

> And argue not with the people of Scripture unless it be in [a way] that is better, ... say: We believe in that which hath been revealed unto us and revealed unto you; our God and your God is one, and unto Him we surrender. (Sura 29:46)

As Muhammad's power increased in Medina, however, he turned on the Jewish tribes and Christians who refused to accept him as the unique prophet of God. Sura 9:5 commands, "Slay the idolaters wherever ye find them, and take them [captive], and besiege them and prepare for them each ambush." Verse 29 adds, "Fight against such of those who have been given the Scripture as believe not in Allah nor the Last Day."

Muhammad confirmed this teaching in the Hadith. "I have been ordered [by Allah] to fight the people till they say: 'None has the right to be worshipped but Allah'" (Hadith 2:483).

LATER REVELATIONS THAT
ANNUL EARLIER REVELATIONS

According to Quranic teaching, Allah can change His mind and replace a verse with a later and better revelation.

Such of our revelations as we abrogate our cause to be forgotten, we bring [in place] one better or the like thereof. Knowest thou not that Allah is able to do all things? (Sura 2:106)

And when we put a revelation in place of [another] revelation— and Allah knowest best what He revealest. (Sura 16:101)

Militant Muslims say that the later revelations, as in Sura 9:5, 29, annul the earlier revelations (Sura 2:62, 256) that were tolerant of non-Muslims. These later Quranic suras justify *jihad,* that is, war on infidels.

DIFFERENCES BETWEEN MUHAMMAD'S
LIFE IN MECCA AND MEDINA

When Muhammad began receiving revelations in A.D. 610, the people of Mecca tolerated the various creeds espoused in Arabia. As long as Muhammad kept to general statements, such as exhortations to live good lives, his preaching continued to be accepted. When Muhammad began to attack the idolatry of the Kaaba (see glossary), active opposition began. He attracted only a small number of followers, and soon the time came to try another city. The words ". . . and turn aside from those who join gods with Allah" (Sura 6:106) are said to be a command from Allah to leave Mecca after preaching there for thirteen years. Muhammad and his one hundred fifty followers journeyed to Medina in 622.

Mark A. Gabriel, former professor of Islamic history at al-Azhar University of Cairo, Egypt, notes that Muhammad, while living in Mecca, "never spoke of *jihad*." He did not mention a "holy war" because he lacked the military might. While in Medina, however, where he built an army,

> the major topic of Quranic revelation was *jihad* and fighting the enemy. . . . Let's compare the differences between Muhammad's life in Mecca and his life in Medina.
>
> - Mecca: He invited people to be part of Islam by preaching.
>   Medina: He persuaded people to convert by the sword.
> - Mecca: He acted like a priest living a life of prayer, fasting, and worship.
>   Medina: He behaved like a military commander, personally leading twenty-seven attacks.
> - Mecca: He had only one wife, Khadija, for those twelve years.
>   Medina: He married twelve more women in ten years.

- Mecca: He fought against idol worship.
  Medina: He fought against People of the Book (Jews and Christians).

Muhammad's move from Mecca to Medina changed Islam into a political movement.[1]

BASIC FACTS ABOUT THE QURAN

Here are some basic facts about the structure of the Quran, Muhammad's role in its writing, and the Quran's revered position among Muslims.

- The Quran was reputedly revealed in Arabic over a period of twenty-two years (610–632).
- The arrangement of the 114 suras is not chronological. The longest suras are placed first in the Quran.
- According to Theodore Nöldeke's *Geschichte des Qorans* (*History of the Quorons*), ninety suras (chapters) were revealed while Muhammad was in Mecca and twenty-four suras while he was in Medina.[2]
- Sura 96 is said to be the first sura revealed to Muhammad.
- Sura 1 (the Fatiha) is often described as "the essence of the Quran."
- The "mother of the Quran" (Ummu-L-Kitab) is said to be in heaven, written by Allah Himself.
- Muslims say that the angel Gabriel revealed the Quran to Muhammad.
- The Quran is considered an integral part of Allah's being. It was not created. Starting in A.D. 610, Muslims believe there was a telling forth of that which always was.

- The third caliph, Uthman (644–656), established the official text of the Quran and had other texts burned.

Two Abodes: Abode of Islam and the Abode of War

Islam divides the peoples of the world into two distinct realms or abodes: the Abode of Islam and the Abode of War. The former have submitted to the will of Allah, and the latter are still resisting. Countries under Muslim control are considered the Abode of Islam. It is the duty of all Muslims to preserve the Abode of Islam from contamination and, where possible, to enlarge it at the expense of the Abode of War, where the "infidel" rules.

Many Muslims believe that the nations of the West established Israel in the heart of the Arab world to be the outpost of their civilization, to be a sword of the West hanging over the necks of Muslims. Therefore, many militant Muslims are committed to restoring Israel's territory to Muslim control and to preserve the Abode of Islam in Palestine. Islam teaches that Muslims who die in the struggle against infidels will immediately be translated to paradise.

Muhammad: The Final and Greatest Prophet

Muslims believe that Jesus' limited ministry was to announce the messenger who would follow him, that is, Ahmad (a variant of Muhammad): "Jesus son of Mary said . . . 'I am the messenger of Allah . . . bringing good tidings of a messenger who cometh after me, whose name is the Praised One [Ahmad]' " (Sura 61:6).

Therefore, Muslims regard Muhammad as the final and greatest prophet. "Muhammad is the messenger of Allah and the Seal of the Prophets" (Sura 33:40). They consider Muhammad (or Ahmad) to be unique because Allah revealed His perfect revelation, the Quran, to Muhammad. Muhammad was the channel through whom the will of Allah became known. Muslims believe the miracle of the Quran proves that Muhammad is the final prophet.

A more detailed discussion of the role of Muhammad as the great prophet can be found in chapter 2, in the section "Prophets."

WAR AND PEACE ACCORDING TO TWO PROPHETS

Jesus Christ and Muhammad, leaders of two great world religions, are both thought to advocate peace, but their goals and approaches differ markedly. The chart "Differences in the Teachings of Jesus and Muhammad" points out those differences.

Differences in the Teachings of Jesus and Muhammad

JESUS	MUHAMMAD
■ Jesus declared, "Blessed are the peacemakers" (Matthew 5:9). His words inspired followers to seek peace with all people (see also 1 Peter 3:11). They certainly did not promote His followers to harm people who did not accept His teachings.	■ Allah told Muhammad: "Fight against such of those who have been given the Scripture as believe not in Allah nor the Last Day" (Sura 9:29). This verse inspires militant Muslims to fight people who do not accept the religion of Islam.

JESUS

- In essence, Jesus said, "Believe and live." He declared, "I am the resurrection and the life. He who believes in me will live, even though he dies; and whoever lives and believes in me will never die" (John 11:25–26).

- Jesus accepted the fact that some of His followers would no longer follow Him because of His teaching (see John 6:60–66). In Christianity, turning away from the faith is not considered a crime.

- Jesus' mission was to conquer sin's penalty and power by His vicarious death. "God made him who had no sin to be sin for us, so that in him we might become the righteousness of God" (2 Corinthians 5:21; see also 1 Peter 3:18).

MUHAMMAD

- In essence, Muhammad said, "Convert or die." He declared, "I have been ordered [by Allah] to fight the people till they say: None has the right to be worshipped but Allah, and whoever said it then he will save his life and property" (Hadith 2:483).

- Muhammad taught his followers to kill anyone who left the faith: ". . . the statement of Allah's Apostle, 'Whoever changed his Islamic religion, then kill him'" (Hadith 9:57).

- Muhammad's mission was to conquer the world for Allah. The goal of jihad, or a holy war, is to establish Islamic authority over the whole world. Islam teaches that Allah is the only authority, and all political systems must be based on Allah's teaching. Allah is important.

Notice that much of the call to action comes in the Hadith, a companion book that amplifies on the Quran by quoting the words of Muhammad. Islam teaches that man's success on this earth and in the hereafter depends on obeying the teachings in the Quran. In the Quran is found a code for all of man's life, including the place of war and peace in one's life. The broad examples of life in the Quran become specific as a Muslim follows the example of Muhammad. The Quran says, "Verily in the messenger of Allah ye have a good example for him who looketh unto Allah and the Last Day, and remembereth Allah much" (Sura 33:21). But important words of Allah's messenger are found in the Hadith.

MUHAMMAD AND THE HADITH

Muslims are greatly affected by the Hadith, which is a record of the sayings and deeds of Muhammad. These styles of behavior have been passed down for thirteen hundred years. In the Hadith, Muhammad is seen in "the ordinary acts of his life—sleeping, eating, mating, praying, dispensing justice, planning, expeditions and revenge against his enemies . . . morality derives from the Prophet's actions; the moral is whatever he did. Morality does not determine the Prophet's actions, but his actions determine and define morality. Muhammad's acts were not ordinary acts; they were Allah's own acts."[3]

Muslims seeking to gain Allah's favor are to follow the styles of behavior in Muhammad's everyday life. Therefore, to be as good as Muhammad is the ideal of every Muslim. Muhammad's teaching became the dogma of Islam. In *Unveiling Islam,* Ergun and Emir Caner note:

> According to the South African Council of Muslim Theologians, the Hadith/Sunnah is the sensible explanation of an otherwise ambiguous Quran. They explain, "The Holy

Quran without the Hadith or Sunnah of the Prophet remains unintelligible in certain instances and in view of that,
the Holy Quran has, in several verses, ordered Muslims to
follow the Prophet in all his deeds and sayings. Therefore, if
one believes in the Holy Quran, there is no alternative but
to uphold the Hadith of the Prophet."[4]

The most authoritative collection of the Hadith was
put together by Sahih-Al-Bukhari (A.D. 811–876) more
than two hundred years after Muhammad's death. The
nine-volume Arabic-English collection of Al-Bukhari's *Hadith* is 4,705 pages in length. (It is also available on Alim-
ISL software.) This collection of traditions is the Islamic
reference for this book.

Teachings from the Hadith have profound effects on
Muslim lives. For example, Muhammad said in Hadith
9:459 that Allah guarantees anyone who engages in holy
war (jihad) for the cause of jihad alone with "belief in [Al-
lah's] words, that He will either admit him into paradise or
return him with his reward or the booty he has earned to
his residence from where he went out."

As a result, young Muslim men and women, believing
their efforts against America to be a holy war (jihad), believe
they will be admitted to paradise if they die in the process.

Interestingly, the Hadith addresses specific conduct between men and women, husbands and wives, as well as
personal hygiene. (See chapter 3 for specific examples.)
Two traditions govern the conduct of men and women:

Then he heard the Prophet saying, "It is not permissible for a man
to be alone with a woman, and no lady should travel except with a
Muhram, i.e, her husband or a person whom she cannot marry."
(4:250)

The prophet said: "None of you should flog his wife as he flogs a slave and then have sexual intercourse with her in the last part of the day." (7:132)

HADITH FOLLOWED RATHER THAN THE QURAN

Sometimes fundamentalist Muslim authorities follow the Hadith rather than the Quran. In a way, teachings of the Hadith can supersede those of the Quran. For example, in Sura 4:15–16 persons guilty of fornication are to be confined to the house until death takes them. Sura 24:2 says, "The adulterer and the adulteress, scourge ye each one of them [with] a hundred stripes." The Quran never says that sexual sins are to be punished by stoning the guilty parties. However, Muhammad and his disciples enforced this extreme penalty.

Thus, stoning in public is still carried out in some Muslim countries, based on Hadith 8:816, which says, "We do not find the verses of [stoning to death] in the Holy Book. . . . Lo! I confirm that the penalty of Rajam [stoning] be inflicted on him who commits illegal sexual intercourse. . . . Allah's Apostle carried out the penalty of Rajam, and so did we after him."

Even though Muhammad died almost fourteen hundred years ago, his sayings and acts are still considered "rigid guidance" and affect more than one billion Muslims. The Hadith shows how to put the guidance of the Quran into practice. The Hadith itself declares: "Abdullah said, 'The best talk is Allah's Book [Quran] and the best guidance is the guidance of Muhammad'" (8:120).

Muslims feel close to Muhammad in his life and hope to be closer in paradise. They follow Islam, a seventh-century religious system that still governs believers' everyday lives.

A Chronology of Biblical and Islamic World Events

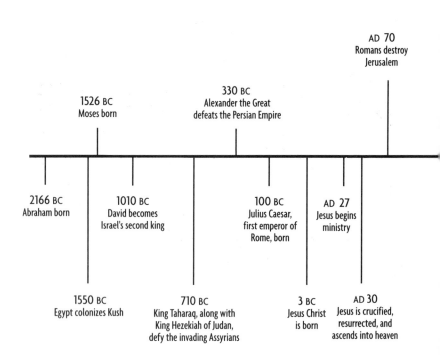

AD 70
Romans destroy
Jerusalem

1526 BC
Moses born

330 BC
Alexander the Great
defeats the Persian Empire

2166 BC
Abraham born

1010 BC
David becomes
Israel's second king

100 BC
Julius Caesar,
first emperor of
Rome, born

AD 27
Jesus begins
ministry

1550 BC
Egypt colonizes Kush

710 BC
King Taharaq, along with
King Hezekiah of Judan,
defy the invading Assyrians

3 BC
Jesus Christ
is born

AD 30
Jesus is crucified,
resurrected, and
ascends into heaven

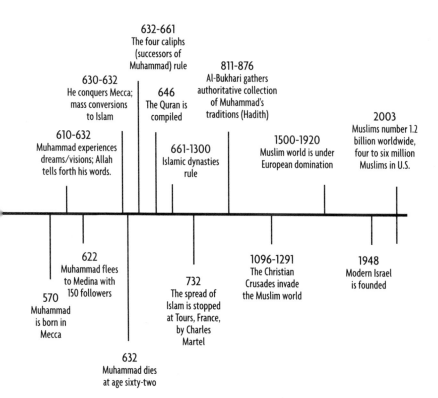

632-661
The four caliphs
(successors of
Muhammad) rule

811-876
Al-Bukhari gathers
authoritative collection
of Muhammad's
traditions (Hadith)

630-632
He conquers Mecca;
mass conversions
to Islam

646
The Quran is
compiled

2003
Muslims number 1.2
billion worldwide,
four to six million
Muslims in U.S.

610-632
Muhammad experiences
dreams/visions; Allah
tells forth his words.

661-1300
Islamic dynasties
rule

1500-1920
Muslim world is under
European domination

622
Muhammad flees
to Medina with
150 followers

1096-1291
The Christian
Crusades invade
the Muslim world

1948
Modern Israel
is founded

570
Muhammad
is born in
Mecca

732
The spread of
Islam is stopped
at Tours, France,
by Charles
Martel

632
Muhammad dies
at age sixty-two

SIGNIFICANT DIFFERENCES BETWEEN CHRISTIANITY AND ISLAM

M any differences exist between Christianity and Islam. Yet before exploring those differences, we should recognize that some basic convictions are common to both faiths.

Indeed, some teaching in the Quran confirms biblical truth. Note these seven truths about God embraced by followers of Islam and Christianity alike:

1. God is one. "Hear, O Israel: The LORD our God, the LORD is one" (Deuteronomy 6:4; supported in Sura 4:171).
2. God is the great and sovereign Creator. "In the beginning God created the heavens and the earth" (Genesis 1:1; supported in Sura 50:38).
3. God revealed His will through the prophets and

apostles. "And so was fulfilled what the Lord had said through the prophet: 'Out of Egypt I called my son'" (Matthew 2:15; supported in Sura 16:36).

4. God wants to forgive! He is full of mercy and kindness. "For the LORD your God is a merciful God" (Deuteronomy 4:31; supported in Sura 2:218).

5. All creation has the privilege and duty to worship God. "All the earth bows down to you; they sing praise to you" (Psalm 66:4; supported in Sura 1:4).

6. God controls history. All men will be judged. "For God will bring every deed into judgment" (Ecclesiastes 12:14; supported in Sura 1:3).

7. We can bring our requests to God in prayer. "Do not be anxious about anything, but in everything, by prayer and petition, with thanksgiving present your requests to God" (Philippians 4:6; supported in Sura 2:153).

Notice the common beliefs among Muslims and Christians. We agree that God is one, God rules, God reveals His will; we believe God judges, is merciful, and forgives. Yet Muslims and Christians disagree on exactly *how* God creates, rules, reveals His will, judges, loves, and forgives. Indeed, the partial truth that Muslims have of God blinds them to the full truth.

DIFFERENCES IN THE NATURE OF GOD

In *The Meaning of the Holy Quran,* Abdullah Yusuf Ali has listed eighty-eight attributes of Allah. The important attributes that are noted in the Bible—God is righteous, God is just, God is faithful, and God is loving—are all missing.

The psalmist wrote, "Righteousness and justice are the foundation of your throne; love and faithfulness go before you" (Psalm 89:14). These attributes form the fundamental aspects of who the God of the Bible is and how He rules. Yet this is not the picture we have of Allah.

The essence and attributes of Allah differ notably from those of God. The following chart notes the fundamental differences between the Deity described in Christianity and Judaism and the deity of Islam.

The Essence and Attributes of God

CHRISTIANITY	ISLAM
▪ Righteousness and justice are parts of the holiness of God that are seen in His treatment of His creatures. God will never do anything that is not morally perfect. "For the LORD is righteous, he loves justice" (Psalm 11:7).	▪ There is no law of righteousness in the being of Allah. He does as He pleases, guiding some men aright and others astray. Allah created some men and spirits to send them to hell: ". . . that I will fill hell with the jinn and mankind together" (Sura 32:13).
▪ God loves all mankind. "For God so loved the world that he gave his one and only Son" (John 3:16). "God is love" (1 John 4:8).	▪ Allah has no affection or feeling for any creature. Love is conditional to those who believe and do good works. "Lo! those who believe and do good works, the Beneficient will appoint for them love" (Sura 19:96).

CHRISTIANITY	ISLAM
■ God is always faithful to His covenants and doesn't change His mind. "The LORD your God is God; he is the faithful God, keeping his covenant of love to a thousand generations" (Deuteronomy 7:9). "The Father . . . does not change" (James 1:17).	■ Allah does not make covenants with man. He can and does change His mind. "And when we put a revelation in place of [another] revelation—and Allah knowest best what He revealeth" (Sura 16:101).

Two Muslim philosophers, Al-Ghazali and Resalah-L-Berkawi, give insights into the Muslim understanding of Allah. Al-Ghazali says, "It is inconceivable that Allah should love mankind, because where there is love there must be a lover, a sense of incompleteness, a realization that the beloved is needed for complete realization of self. . . . This is impossible with Allah, since Allah is perfectly complete."[1]

Resalah-L-Berkawi says, "If all infidels became believers, He [God] would gain nothing. If all believers became infidels, He would suffer no loss."[2]

Concerning Allah's moral attributes, Samuel M. Zwemer has noted,

While we find that the "terrible" attributes of God's power occur again and again in the Koran, the net moral attributes are found in two verses, which mention that Allah is Holy and Truthful, i.e., in the Moslem sense of those words. What a contrast with the Bible! The Koran shows and Tradition illustrates that Mohammad had in measure a correct idea of the physical attributes (I use the word in a theological sense) of Deity; but he had a false conception of His moral attributes or no conception at all. He saw God's power in nature, but never had a glimpse of His holiness and justice. The reason is plain. Mohammad has no true idea of the nature of sin and its consequences.[3]

Unity and Trinity[4]

CHRISTIANITY	ISLAM
■ God is triune (one God is three persons: Father, Son, and Holy Spirit). These three persons are bound together in a relationship of love, not as three distinct "gods." "The LORD our God, the LORD is one" (Deuteronomy 6:4).	■ Allah is unitary, without persons, "so believe in Allah and His messengers, and say not Three—Cease! [it is] better for you! Allah is one God. For is it removed from His transcendent majesty that He should have a son" (Sura 4:171).
■ The Father is recognized as God. "The Son of Man [Jesus] . . . On him God the Father has placed his seal of approval" (John 6:27).	■ No devout Muslim would call the God of Muhammad "Father," for Muslims consider Allah to be utterly transcendent and unknowable.
■ The Son is recognized as God. "In the beginning was the Word, and the Word was with God, and the Word was God. . . . The Word became flesh" (John 1:1, 14).	■ Muslims believe that Allah created Jesus in the likeness of Adam. "Lo! the likeness of Jesus with Allah is as the likeness of Adam. He created him [Jesus] of dust, then He said unto him: Be! And he is" (Sura 3:59).

CHRISTIANITY

■ Jesus Christ is the second person in the Godhead. "... his Son Jesus Christ. He is the true God and eternal life" (1 John 5:20).

■ The Holy Spirit is God. "You have lied to the Holy Spirit.... You have not lied to men but to God" (Acts 5:3–4).

■ God is Spirit. "God is spirit, and his worshipers must worship in spirit and in truth" (John 4:24).

ISLAM

■ Many Muslims mistakenly believe that the Trinity is God, Mary, and Jesus. "And when Allah saith: O Jesus, son of Mary! Didst thou say unto mankind: Take me and my mother for two gods beside Allah? He saith: Be glorified! It was not mine to utter that to which I had no right" (Sura 5:116).

■ A holy spirit is mentioned three times in the Quran. "Say: the holy spirit hath revealed it from thy Lord" (Sura 16:102). All Muslim commentators agree that the holy spirit means the angel Gabriel.

■ Allah is neither a person nor spirit. There is nothing whatever like unto Him. "Naught is as His likeness; and He is the Hearer, the Seer" (Sura 42:11).

CHRISTIANITY	ISLAM
▪ God has revealed Himself. "No one has ever seen God, but God the One and Only, who is at the Father's side, has made him known" (John 1:18). "In the past God spoke to our forefathers through the prophets . . . but in these last days he has spoken to us by his Son" (Hebrews 1:1–2).	▪ Allah is close with us by His knowledge, not by His personal self. God is completely "other."

The Islamic conception of God the Father, God the Son, and God the Holy Spirit destroys all the basic truths of the Christian faith, leaving no Christian faith at all. Thus Zwemer wrote, "Islam, instead of being a progressive and completed idea, goes to a lower level than the religion it claims to supplant. 'Mohammad teaches a God above us; Moses teaches a God above us and with us; Jesus Christ teaches God above us, God with us, and God in us.'"[5]

Zwemer clarified that "God [is] above us, not as an Oriental despot, but as a heavenly Father. God with us, Emmanuel, in the mystery of His Incarnation, is the stumbling block to the Moslem. God in us through His Spirit renewing the heart and controlling the will into a true Islam [submission to Allah's will], or obedient subjection by a living faith."[6]

In *Cross and Crescent,* Colin Chapman wrote, "Islam seems to be saying to the Christian world, 'You've got it all wrong about Jesus! Your Trinity of three persons in one God is impossible to understand, let alone explain. Islam is a simple creed without dogmas and this belief in one

Creator God includes all that had previously been revealed in Judaism and Christianity.' "7

JESUS CHRIST

The differences in the identity of Jesus of Nazareth are many and significant, as noted in the chart "The Identity and Ministry of Jesus Christ."

The Identity and Ministry of Jesus Christ

CHRISTIANITY

■ *Conception.* Mary's child, Jesus, was conceived by the Holy Spirit. "Mary, you have found favor with God. You will be with child and give birth to a son, and you are to give him the name Jesus. . . . The Holy Spirit will come upon you" (Luke 1:30–31, 35).

■ *Divinity.* Jesus affirms that He is the Son of God. "The high priest said to him, 'I charge you under oath by the living God: Tell us if you are the Christ, the Son of God.' 'Yes, it is as you say,' Jesus replied" (Matthew 26:63–64).

ISLAM

■ Jesus Christ was born of the virgin Mary by a special miracle. "O Mary! Lo! Allah hath chosen thee. . . . She said: My Lord! How can I have a child when no mortal has touched me?" (Sura 3:42, 47). The Muslim commentator Zamakhshari says the virgin conceived "when the angel Gabriel blew up her garment."8

■ Jesus speaks from the cradle, saying He is a prophet (slave of Allah), negating that He is the Son of God. "How can we talk to the one who is in the cradle, a young boy? He spake: Lo! I am the slave of Allah. He hath given me the Scriptures and hath appointed me a Prophet" (Sura 19:29–30).

CHRISTIANITY

- *Nature.* Jesus committed no sin. He lived a perfect life. "Christ suffered for you . . . 'He committed no sin'" (1 Peter 2:21–22).

- *Miracles.* Jesus healed the sick and raised the dead (all by His power). "'But that you may know that the Son of Man [Jesus] has authority on earth to forgive sins . . . .' He said to the paralytic, 'I tell you, get up, take your mat and go home.' He got up" (Mark 2:10–12).

- *Ministry.* Jesus completed the work God had given Him. "Father, the time has come. Glorify your Son, that your Son may glorify you. . . . I have brought you glory on earth by completing the work you gave me to do" (John 17:1, 4).

ISLAM

- Jesus was considered righteous, along with others. ". . . John and Jesus and Elias. Each one [of them] was of the righteous" (Sura 6:86).

- Jesus Christ healed the sick, raised the dead, and made a clay pigeon become alive. All were done with Allah's permission. "When Allah saith: O Jesus . . . thou didst shape of clay as it were the likeness of a bird . . . heal him who was born blind and the leper . . . raise the dead, by my permission" (Sura 5:110).

- Jesus' life and ministry were inferior to those of earlier prophets as well as those of Muhammad. Sura 13:38 states that Allah had designated wives and children for all His prophets. The exception was Jesus. His ministry lasted only three years.

CHRISTIANITY

■ *His Messenger.* Jesus taught that the Holy Spirit would come after His death and resurrection. "And I will ask the Father, and he will give you another Counselor to be with you forever . . . the Counselor, the Holy Spirit, whom the Father will send in my name" (John 14:16, 26).

■ *Death.* Jesus Christ died on the cross as the perfect sacrifice for sin. As foretold in Isaiah 53:6, "The LORD has laid on him the iniquity of us all." "The Christ had to suffer and rise from the dead" (Acts 17:3).

■ *Resurrection.* Jesus Christ rose from the dead after three days. "Christ died for our sins according to the Scriptures, that he was buried, that he was raised on the third day" (1 Corinthians 15:3–4).

ISLAM

■ Jesus' limited ministry was to announce the messenger who would follow him, Ahmad (a variant of Muhammad). "Jesus son of Mary said . . . I am the messenger of Allah . . . bringing good tidings of a messenger who cometh after me, whose name is the Praised One [Ahmad]" (Sura 61:6).

■ Jesus did not die; someone else died in His place. "They slew him not nor crucified, but it appeared so unto them" (Sura 4:157).

■ God took Jesus to paradise as He had done with Enoch and Elijah. "But Allah took him unto Himself" (Sura 4:158).

CHRISTIANITY

■ *Authority.* Jesus has been given all authority in heaven and earth. He rules and expands His kingdom from heaven. "Jesus Christ, who has gone into heaven and is at God's right hand—with angels, authorities and powers in submission to him" (1 Peter 3:21–22).

■ *Intercession.* Jesus has become a High Priest, interceding for His followers. "Because Jesus lives forever, he has a permanent priesthood. . . . He always lives to intercede for them" (Hebrews 7:24–25).

ISLAM

■ Jesus does not rule. Only Allah has this power.

■ Jesus humbly indicates His inability to function as intercessor. "Allah's Apostle said, 'Allah will gather all people on the Day of Resurrection and they will say, "Let us request someone to intercede for us with our Lord." . . . They will go to him [Jesus], and he will say, "I am not fit for this undertaking, go to Muhammad"'" (Hadith 8:570).

CHRISTIANITY

■ *Return.* Jesus will return from heaven to earth to rule forever. "Jesus Christ . . . the ruler of the kings of the earth. . . . Look, he is coming with the clouds" (Revelation 1:5–7).

■ *Judgment.* When Jesus returns, He will judge the living and the dead. "When the Lord Jesus is revealed from heaven . . . he will punish those who do not know God" (2 Thessalonians 1:7–8).

ISLAM

■ Many Muslim scholars believe Jesus will return from heaven and punish Jews and Christians for their failure to accept Muhammad as the Prophet. He will help establish Islam as the only religion of the world. "By Him in Whose Hands my soul is, son of Mary [Jesus] will shortly descend amongst you people [Muslims] as a just ruler and will break the Cross and kill the pig" (Hadith 3:425).

■ Jesus will judge the people by the Law of the Quran. "Allah's Apostle said, 'How will you be when the son of Mary descends amongst you and he will judge people by the Law of the Quran and not by the Law of the Gospel?'" (Hadith 4:658).

In *Christian Ethics,* Isma'il Ragi al-Faruqi wrote of Islam and its view of redemption: "Just as the revelation of Christ is the redemptive act of God for Christians, so Islam believes that the revelation [to] Muhammad is the redemptive act of God. As the revelation of Christ redeemed man from bondage to sin, so the revelation [to] Muhammad redeemed man from bondage to shirk (associationism [i.e., associating Jesus and the Holy Spirit as partners with God]) and kufr (ungodliness or no faith).[9]

McDowell and Zaka noted that the Quran emphasizes that Jesus never claimed to be a god or the Son of God. Instead, He was only the servant and apostle of the Lord; so were the prophets before Him. They added:

> Even when the [Quran] says that Jesus was a spirit from
> Allah, that is interpreted to mean a soul created by Allah.
> Muslims are confounded by the relationship between the
> Father and the Son in the Christian Godhead. How can
> Jesus, a man, be God? The assumption behind this question
> is that Jesus, in Christian theology, somehow became God.
> It is thought that Jesus' followers gave him this divine status. But, according to the Scriptures, Jesus has always been
> God from the beginning (John 1:1).[10]

THE HOLY SPIRIT

Islam identifies the person and work of the Holy Spirit much differently than Christianity does, as the chart on the following page shows.

Differences in Understanding of the Holy Spirit

CHRISTIANITY

■ The Holy Spirit is God and has all the attributes of God. "You have lied to the Holy Spirit. . . . You have not lied to men but to God" (Acts 5:3–4).

■ He is a person who is the Convictor, Convincer, and Converter of sinners. "The Counselor . . . will convict the world of guilt . . . and righteousness and judgment" (John 16:7–8).

■ The Spirit of God indwells believers in Christ, guides them, and empowers them to be more like Christ. "By the Spirit you put to death the misdeeds of the body. . . . [You] are led by the Spirit of God" (Romans 8:13–14).

ISLAM

■ The Holy Spirit is the angel of revelation, Gabriel. "We gave Jesus . . . clear proofs [of Allah's sovereignty] and we supported him with the holy spirit" (Sura 2:253). Muslim commentators agree this passage refers to the angel Gabriel.

■ The Spirit is God's own breath. "So, when I have made him [Adam] and have breathed into him of My Spirit" (Sura 15:29).

■ Allah guides man by His law. There is no spiritual indwelling and no empowering.

CHRISTIANITY

- The Holy Spirit inspired men to write the Scriptures. "Men spoke from God as they were carried along by the Holy Spirit" (2 Peter 1:21).

- The indwelling Spirit of God allows fellowship with God. "Don't you know that you yourselves are God's temple and that God's Spirit lives in you?" (1 Corinthians 3:16).

ISLAM

- The Scriptures were written by God and sent down to man. "Adam said to . . . Moses, Allah favored you with His talk and He wrote [the Torah] for you with His own hand" (Hadith 8:611).

- Allah has no fellowship with man, who was not created in the image of Allah.

Many Christians say that "God is a spirit," citing Jesus' words in John 4:24. However, when Muslims hear that, they "believe that we are speaking a horrible blasphemy. The Quran does use the word spirit twenty times, but each time the word is understood to refer to a created being that has a subtle body capable of penetrating a coarse body. Angels and jinn have such subtle bodies. So to say God is a spirit is understood to mean that he is a created being."[11]

Muslims maintain that Muhammad is the Paraclete (Counselor, Comforter, Advocate) promised in the gospel of John, chapters 14–16. They quote Sura 61:6, which states: "And when Jesus son of Mary said: 'O Children of Israel! Lo! I am the messenger of Allah unto you, and bring good tidings of a messenger who cometh after me, whose name is the Praised One [Muhammad].'"

Muslims try to substantiate their claim that Muhammad

(or Ahmad, sometimes spelled *Ahmed*) is the promised Paraclete by offering this argument:

> The Greek word from which the word "Comforter" comes is "Paracletos," which Muslims assert is a corruption of the original word "Periclutos" which you will note is a change of two vowels. The word "Periclutos" is said to mean "Praise" and is translated in the Arabic language as "AL HAMD." This you will observe has three consonants 'H-M-D.' These are the consonants of the nouns Ahmed and Muhammed, so the Muslims claim that Jesus said, "after me I will send the praised one . . . AHMED, and he shall guide you into all truth,' etc."[12]

In John 14:26, the Counselor is identified as the Holy Spirit. "But the Counselor, the Holy Spirit, whom the Father will send in my name, will teach you all things and will remind you of everything I have said to you." Only the Holy Spirit could remain with them forever and live in believers. These verses suggest no reference to Muhammad. For this omission, Muslims charge that Christians have changed the Bible.

GOD, CREATION, AND MAN'S FALL

Fundamental differences exist in the accounts of the world's creation and mankind's fall into sin.

The Creation and the Fall into Sin

CHRISTIANITY

■ God created all things through His Word, who is Jesus Christ. "Through him [the Word] all things were made. . . . He was in the world, and . . . the world was made through him" (John 1:3, 10).

■ God created all things in six days and rested on the seventh day. "By the seventh day God had finished the work he had been doing; so on the seventh day he rested from all his work" (Genesis 2:2).

■ God made man in His own image, i.e., capable of fellowship with God. "Then God said, 'Let us make man in our image. . . .' So God created man in his own image" (Genesis 1:26–27).

ISLAM

■ Muslims strongly deny that God created all things through Jesus Christ.

■ Allah created all things, but He needed no rest. "And verily we created the heavens and the earth, and all that is between them, in six days, and naught of weariness touched us" (Sura 50:38). In Sura 41:9–10, 12, however, the Quran says that it took Allah *eight* days to create the world (2 days + 4 days + 2 days = 8 days). These verses reveal a discrepancy regarding the number of days of creation.

■ No teaching in the Quran states that man was created in the image of God. Man has no ability to have fellowship with God.

CHRISTIANITY

- All that God made was very good (Genesis 1:31).

- Adam and Eve disobeyed God in the garden by eating forbidden fruit. They were expelled from the garden and from God's presence.

- The garden was on earth.

- Since then, each person is born with a sinful nature. (Psalms 14:3, 51:5) and has fallen into a state of moral and spiritual corruption. Man is under judgment and needs salvation (Romans 3:23).

- Fellowship with God was broken because of Adam's sin.

ISLAM

- Allah is the author of good and evil. "Say: I seek refuge in the Lord of Daybreak from the evil of that which He created" (Sura 113:1–2).

- Man had to "go down" from the garden, where he disobeyed Allah. However, he was forgiven and told he had nothing to fear if he followed God's laws.

- The garden was in paradise.

- Adam repented and was forgiven. There was no fall. Each person is born weak but good. Man does not need salvation. "Allah would make the burden light for you, for man was created weak" (Sura 4:28).

- No relationship existed with Allah, so nothing was lost when Adam sinned.

As the authors of *Muslims and Christians at the Table* note, the Quran emphasizes Allah's creative power, and that the moral and material good of the world, as well as its moral and evil, are His creation:

This Muslim teaching can be compared to the Manichacans, who believed that there were two powers in the universe, one being the creator of good and the other of evil. These two creative activities are combined in Allah, so that the doctrine of the unity of Allah is a unified dualism. Allah creates all man's acts, both good and evil, and allows man only the power to appropriate (*iktisab*) the acts that he has created for him.[13]

Muslims believe "man's present state is normal. Created weak and inconstant, Adam simply forgot God's command and nothing changed. Man did not fall, in the moral sense, and hence he does not need salvation. If man will follow God's guidance and faithfully perform His prescriptions, he will again enjoy the garden (heaven) at the resurrection."[14]

GOD AND MANKIND

Looking at the Islamic and Christian Scriptures, it becomes clear that only Christianity teaches that people can have a relationship with God.

The Relationship Between God and Mankind

CHRISTIANITY

- Man can experience personal fellowship with God. "Our fellowship is with the Father and with his Son, Jesus Christ" (1 John 1:3).

ISLAM

- Allah does not have personal relationships with people.

CHRISTIANITY

■ Fellowship with God is hindered by man's sin. "If we claim to have fellowship with him yet walk in the darkness, we lie and do not live by the truth" (1 John 1:6).

■ Whoever calls to God receives a response. God may change the course of events in response to prayer (2 Kings 20:1–6).

■ God reveals Himself by His Son, His Spirit, and His creation. "In these last days he has spoken to us by his Son" (Hebrews 1:2; see also John 15:26; Romans 1:20).

■ God generally prospers those who trust and obey Him. However, He sometimes allows His children and prophets to suffer, but He uses even the suffering for their good (Roman 8:28).

ISLAM

■ Since fellowship is not possible, sin doesn't hinder any relationship.

■ Allah has decreed everything before Creation. He is both the causer and decider of man's fate. Man lives out what Allah has decreed. Everything is written (*maktoob*). "Adam said to him, O Moses . . . do you blame me for action Allah had written in my fate forty years before my creation?" (Hadith 8:611).

■ Allah reveals only by His commands. He does not reveal Himself. "Islam teaches that God does not reveal Himself to anyone in any way. God reveals only His will, which is found in the Quran."[15]

■ Allah prospers those who trust and obey Him.

The Bible teaches that God loves His human creations and deeply desires to have a personal relationship with every person. This relationship, however, is hindered by man's sin. Jesus Christ came to earth to ultimately die for the penalty of people's sins. A person's relationship with God can be restored through obedient faith in Jesus Christ. A follower of Jesus becomes a son or daughter of God.

Islam teaches that God is unlike mankind and is unknowable. Man's separation from God is normal, and he remains a slave of God. There is a huge difference between being a son of God and a slave of God.

This inability to know God is fundamental in Islam. "For Islam, the gulf between the Creator and His creatures is so absolute and uncrossable that a knowledge of God is impossible. They believe that they can know what He is not, and can know His will, but that He Himself is unknowable."[16]

"One might, at first sight, think that this tremendous Autocrat [Allah], this uncontrolled and unsympathizing Power, would be far above anything like passions, desires or inclinations. Yet such is not the case, for He has with respect to His creatures one main feeling and source of action, namely, jealousy of them, lest they should perchance attribute to themselves something of what is His alone, and thus encroach on His all-engrossing Kingdom," wrote Samuel Zwemer. As a result, "He is more ready to punish than reward, to inflict pain more than to bestow pleasure, to ruin than to build. It is His singular satisfaction to make created beings continually feel that they are nothing else than His slaves."[17]

McDowell and Zaka note the contrast of the loving God in the Bible with the God of the Quran who lacks relationship with His beings:

One fails to find in the Quran an emphasis of God's love for us and our obligation to love God and our neighbors as found in the Bible. . . . One can only find a few verses in the Quran that speak of God's love. . . . Al-Wadud, "the Loving" (Sura 11:90), is one of the 99 beautiful names for Allah, but it does not mean that love is part of his character. Love implies a relationship. But Allah is unknowable, Al-Wadud is unknowable. Al-Wadud comes from the verb wadda, which means "kind" and some aspects of "love," but without its full depth of meaning.[18]

MAN'S BASIC PROBLEM

The concept of sin is fundamental to Christianity, whereas Islam describes most people as good though ignorant of their sins. (See the chart "The Problem of Sin.")

The Problem of Sin

CHRISTIANITY

■ Man by nature is a hopeless sinner, unable to obey God. "Everyone has turned away, they have together become corrupt, there is no one who does good, not even one" (Psalm 53:3).

■ Because of his sinful nature and actions, man is unacceptable to God, who is perfect. "For all have sinned and fall short of the glory of God" (Romans 3:23).

ISLAM

■ Man is ignorant, but good, and only needs instruction to obey God fully.

■ Only unbelievers and great sinners are unacceptable to God.

CHRISTIANITY

■ Corrupt man can do nothing to make himself acceptable to perfect God. There is no way for a person to buy eternal life with God. "No man can redeem the life of another or give to God a ransom for him . . . no payment is ever enough" (Psalm 49:7–8).

■ Man needs salvation from his sinful nature. He is unable to free himself; he needs a Savior.

■ Because of man's sinful nature, he is under the sway of Satan. "Put on the full armor of God so that you can take your stand against the devil's schemes" (Ephesians 6:11).

■ The Bible makes no distinction between major and minor sins. Sinful acts include murder, envy, strife, deceit, gossip, slander, arrogance, and adultery (Romans 1:29–30).

ISLAM

■ By faith and good works, one can be acceptable to God. One must work in all areas of his life to follow the Creator so he can gain the pleasures of God.

■ Man can live a good life if he has good guidance.

■ Satan tempts and deceives man to disobey Allah's commands. "He said: 'Now, because Thou hast sent me astray, verily I shall lurk in ambush for them on Thy Right Path'" (Sura 7:16).

■ Major sins in Islam are apostasy (i. e., abandonment of the faith), refusal to be converted to Islam, declaring Muhammad to be a liar, adultery, murder, mistreatment of one's parents, and desertion during jihad. Minor sins are lying, deception, anger, and lust (Sura 4:31; Hadith 4:28).

CHRISTIANITY

■ Jesus said the desire to have sex with someone other than one's spouse is mental adultery, a sin (Matthew 5:27–28).

■ Because man's sin requires a penalty, man is condemned to hell. "Be afraid of the One who can destroy both soul and body in hell" (Matthew 10:28b).

■ God's solution to man's sinful dilemma is Jesus Christ. "For the wages of sin is death, but the gift of God is eternal life in Christ Jesus our Lord" (Romans 6:23).

■ Sin grieves God and breaks communion between a Christian and his holy God (1 John 1:6–7).

ISLAM

■ There is no Islamic law that says evil thoughts are sin.

■ Allah sends to hell whomever He wants. He created a multitude of spirits and men specifically for the purpose of sending to hell. "That I will fill hell with jinn and mankind together" (Sura 32:13).

■ Islam's solution to man's sinful condition is faith in Allah, following His will, and doing good works.

■ Allah is unaffected by sin. He has no fellowship with man.

Islam minimizes the sinfulness of man. Islam teaches that by good works, one can establish his own righteousness before Allah. A Muslim hopes to receive Allah's mercy and forgiveness. Yet, there is no assurance of salvation. In two instances in the Hadith, Allah's loyal apostle, Muhammad, himself yearns that salvation may be his.

Narrated Aisha: I heard the Prophet and listened to him before his death while he was lying supported on his back, and he was saying: "O Allah! Forgive me, and bestow Your Mercy on me, and let me meet the [highest] companions [of the hereafter]." (Hadith 5:715)

Narrated Abu Huraira: I heard Allah's Apostle saying, "By Allah! I ask for Allah's forgiveness and turn to Him in repentance more than seventy times a day." (Hadith 8:319)

Muhammad even confesses in the Hadith that he is unsure what Allah will do on the Day of Judgment: "The Prophet said . . . By Allah, though I am the Apostle of Allah, yet I do not know what Allah will do with me" (Hadith 5:266.)

McDowell and Zaka sum up the Islamic deviation from Christian teaching:

> The holiness of God and the sinfulness of men are two vital omissions in the quranic revelation, from the Christian perspective. These two truths are inseparable and together pose the problem that required as its solution the vicarious sacrifice of the Righteous One in the place of the sinner in order that salvation might be provided for him. If either the holiness of God or the sinfulness of men is reduced or overlooked, the need for salvation by grace disappears and a religion of human works becomes plausible. This is just what we found in Islam.[19]

THE ANSWER

Christianity and Islam differ regarding the means of deliverance from the penalty of sins as well as man's ability to resist sin.

The Way of Salvation

CHRISTIANITY

■ By dying on the cross for man's sin, Jesus Christ offered Himself to God as a perfect sacrifice. "Now he [Jesus Christ] has appeared once for all at the end of the ages to do away with sin by the sacrifice of himself" (Hebrews 9:26).

■ Jesus Christ lived a perfect and sinless life: ". . . Jesus Christ, the Righteous one" (1 John 2:1; see also Luke 23:47; Acts 3:14–15).

■ By accepting Jesus Christ as the perfect, atoning sacrifice for one's sins, a person can be free from the condemnation to hell. "For the wages of sin is death, but the gift of God is eternal life in Christ Jesus our Lord" (Romans 6:23).

ISLAM

■ No sacrifice for sins is necessary. God can forgive whomever He wants. "In accordance with its minimizing of sin, Islam does not emphasize, as does Christianity, the consequences of sin or the hostility of evil to the purposes of God. As a result, the crucifixion of Christ is unnecessary in Islam."[20]

■ Jesus is faultless. "He said, I am only a messenger of thy Lord, that I may bestow on thee [Mary] a faultless son" (Sura 19:19).

■ Every person is fully responsible for his acts; the consequences of a person's acts cannot be transferred to someone else. No one can vicariously atone for another's sins. "Each soul earneth only on its own account, nor doth any laden bear another's load . . ." (Sura 6:164).

CHRISTIANITY

■ By faith in Jesus Christ, man can receive the Holy Spirit to guide him and give him power to resist sin. "You, however, are controlled not by the sinful nature but by the Spirit . . . you put to death the misdeeds of the body" (Romans 8:9, 13).

■ When one accepts Jesus as Savior and Lord, he enters the kingdom and is adopted as a son of God. "Yet to all who received him [Jesus], to those who believed in his name, he gave the right to become children of God" (John 1:12).

■ Jesus taught and exemplified the daily life as God desires it. The Epistles further explain how this life is to be lived. "Your attitude should be the same as that of Christ Jesus" (Philippians 2:5).

ISLAM

■ People can, by their own efforts, free themselves from the power of sin. They rely on individual effort and collective discipline through knowledge to change sinful ways.

■ Man can never become a son of God. However, he becomes more acceptable to God by resisting Satan and living according to the Islamic Law. Salvation is granted to a person who repeats the Creed: "I bear witness that there is no God but God; I bear witness that Muhammad is the Messenger of God"—and lives according to the Islamic Law.

■ Muhammad taught and exemplified daily life as Allah desires it. Muhammad bears witness to the truth. "And those unto whom they cry instead of Him possess no power of intercession, saving him [Muhammad] who beareth witness unto the Truth knowingly" (Sura 43:86).

The Scriptures teach that a holy God is grieved and troubled by the sinful rebellion of men and women He created in His image. God desires that His people share in His holiness. He says, "You are to be holy to me because I, the LORD, am holy" (Leviticus 20:26).

God cannot easily forgive sin because it offends Him deeply. Jesus Christ, the eternal Son of God, paid the penalty for our sins by dying on the cross. Man, by obedient faith in Jesus Christ, becomes completely acceptable to God and is spiritually born into God's family.

In sharp contrast, Islam teaches that sin does not offend God deeply. Therefore God can readily forgive sins.

> In Muslim theology, there is a sense in which God can forgive easily because sin does not affect him deeply. How could the Almighty God be troubled by the trifling mistakes of a mere mortal? Yet, in the Bible, God is described as becoming troubled—deeply troubled—by the sinful rebellion of the men and women he made in his image. He is offended and grieved by their sins. . . . But what is truly astounding is this: Though God's eyes "are too pure to look on evil" (Habakkuk 1:13), he does not remain aloof from the world, isolated in the splendor of his holiness. He is the Holy One "among you," as Isaiah says (Isaiah 12:6). More astounding still is this: God wants his people to share in his own holiness.[21]

The Allah of the Quran forgives man based on his doing good works and obeying Islamic Law. There is no promise of heaven, because Allah will decide who He will forgive and who He will punish. Only Muslims killed doing jihad, or holy war, are promised to go straight to heaven.

McDowell and Zaka summarize the Muslims' hope of

salvation well: "Although everyone is concerned to avoid hell and make it to heaven, God readily forgives sin. . . . Subhanan Allah ["Glory to God"] and Allahu Akbar ["God is most great"] are often repeated in prayer; their repetition is said to wipe out sins. Doing good deeds also brings forgiveness for sins."[22]

ANGELS AND SATAN

Muslims and Christians agree that angels and Satan exist and are active in this world. But in the Quran, the interactions differ from those described in the Bible. (See the chart "Who Are the Angels?")

Who Are the Angels?

CHRISTIANITY	ISLAM
■ God created angels as spirit beings with supernatural powers. "Are not all angels ministering spirits sent to serve those who will inherit salvation?" (Hebrews 1:14).	■ Allah created angels from light.
■ Some angels left their proper abode and sinned. Satan was the leader in this apostasy. "For if God did not spare angels when they sinned . . ." (2 Peter 2:4). "You [Satan] said in your heart, 'I will ascend to heaven. . . . I will make myself like the Most High" (Isaiah 14:13–14).	■ There are fallen angels, the chief of which is Satan (called Iblis). Satan refused to fall prostrate before Adam. "And we created you, then fashioned you, then told the angels: Fall ye prostrate before Adam! And they fell prostrate, all save Iblis. . . . Iblis said: I am better than him" (Sura 7:11–12).

CHRISTIANITY

■ Since Satan cannot attack God directly, he attacks God's master creation, man. "Be self-controlled and alert. Your enemy the devil prowls around . . . looking for someone to devour" (1 Peter 5:8).

■ Satan accuses Christ's brethren of their shortcomings before God. "The devil, or Satan . . . the accuser of our brothers . . . accuses them before our God" (Revelation 12:9–10).

■ Ultimately, Satan will be defeated. "The devil . . . was thrown into the lake of burning sulfur" (Revelation 20:10).

■ Demons and unclean spirits seek to possess men (Matthew 8:16).

■ The archangel Michael protects and prospers Israel (Daniel 12:1). The archangel Gabriel announced to Mary the birth of the Savior.

ISLAM

■ Satan enticed Adam to disobey Allah. "And we said: O Adam! Dwell thou and thy wife in the Garden . . . but Satan caused them to deflect there from" (Sura 2:35–36).

■ Satan entices men not to believe. "Because Thou hast sent me astray, verily I shall lurk in ambush for them on Thy Right Path" (Sura 7:16).

■ Daily recitation from the Quran is believed to keep Satan away from the home.

■ There are jinn, who may be evil spirits (demons) or good spirits (Hadith 1:450).

■ In Islam, the four angels with names are: Gabriel (Jibril), who brought the Quran to Muhammad; Michael, who watches over the world; Israfil, who will sound the trumpet at the last judgment; and Izrail, who is the angel of death.

CHRISTIANITY

ISLAM

■ Good angels protect and deliver God's people. "He will command his angels . . . to guard you in all your ways" (Psalm 91:11).

■ Ministering angels include the recording angels (of good and bad deeds—Sura 50:17–18) and questioners of the dead.

Religion is generally defined as "interactions between humans and the supernatural." The following are some references to the supernatural world in the Hadith (the sayings and actions of Muhammad):

- *Divine Revelation Revealed.* "Al-Harith bin Hisham asked Allah's Apostle [Muhammad], 'O Allah's Apostle! How is the Divine Inspiration revealed to you?' Allah's Apostle replied, 'Sometimes it is [revealed] like the ringing of a bell, this form of Inspiration is the hardest of all. . . . Sometimes the Angel [Gabriel] comes to me in the form of a man and talks to me'" (Hadith 1:2). Later in Hadith we read, "He heard Allah's Apostle describing . . . the Divine Inspiration . . . 'while I was walking, I heard a voice from the sky and behold! I saw the same Angel who came to me in the cave at Hira,' sitting on a chair between the sky and the earth" (6:448).
- *Angels Quiz the Dead.* According to Hadith 2:422, the Prophet said, "When a human is laid in his grave . . . two angels come to him and make him sit and ask him 'What did you used to say about this man, Muhammad?' He will say 'I testify that he is Allah's slave and Apostle.' Then it will be said to him, 'Look at your place in the Hell-Fire. Allah has given you a place in Paradise instead of it.'"

- *Satan's Activity.* The Prophet once offered a prayer and said, "Satan came in front of me and tried to interrupt my prayer, but Allah gave me an upper hand on him and I choked him" (Hadith 2:301). Satan also causes newborns to cry at his touch (6:71), and his "devils spread out at nightfall" (7:527). Satan even affects the animals and our dream life:

> The Prophet said, "When you hear the crowing of cocks, ask for Allah's Blessings for [their crowing indicates that] they have seen an angel. And when you hear the braying of donkeys, seek refuge with Allah from Satan . . . they have seen Satan." (Hadith 4:522)

> The Prophet said, "A good dream is from Allah, and a bad dream is from Satan." (Hadith 9:124)

- *Angels Ask Allah's Forgiveness.* Allah's apostle said, "The angels keep on asking Allah's forgiveness for anyone of you, as long as he is at his Musalla [praying place] and he does not Hadath [expel gas]" (Hadith 1:436).

THE PROPHETS

The differences in beliefs about the identity and role of prophets is significant: Christianity subordinates all prophets to Jesus, while Islam elevates Muhammad above all prophets. Muhammad is declared above Jesus, who is Himself only a prophet, according to Islamic teaching. (See the chart "Who Are the Prophets?")

Who Are the Prophets?

CHRISTIANITY

- The prophet has a clear call from God at the beginning of his ministry.

- God calls a prophet to speak His message to people.

- A prophet is inspired by God but uses his own language to deliver the message.

- Prophets are attested by miracles (such as healings) and foretelling events that come to pass. "The prophets, who through faith conquered kingdoms . . . shut the mouths of lions, quenched the fury of the flames, and escaped the edge of the sword" (Hebrews 11:32–34).

ISLAM

- A prophet/messenger is sent with divine Scripture to guide erring man in his path.

- When the teaching of a prophet is distorted by people, Allah sends another prophet to bring humans back to the straight path. The chain of prophets began with Adam and included Noah, Abraham, Ishmael, Isaac, Moses, David, and Jesus; the final prophet was Muhammad.

- Allah in mercy sent many prophets to all the nations. "And verily we have raised in every nation a messenger [proclaiming], Serve Allah and shun false gods" (Sura 16:36).

- The four most important prophets are Moses, David, Jesus, and Muhammad. Each was given a holy book from Allah. Muslims consider Jesus to be a great prophet (Sura 2:253).

CHRISTIANITY

■ God has spoken in these last days by His Son. "In the past God spoke to our forefathers through the prophets at many times and in various ways, but in these last days he has spoken to us by his Son" (Hebrews 1:1–2).

■ Some prophets were put to death. "[The prophets] were tortured . . . faced jeers and flogging . . . [were] put in prison . . . [and] put to death" (Hebrews 11:32, 35–37).

■ Jesus affirms that He is the Son of God. "The high priest said to him, 'I charge you under oath by the living God: Tell us if you are the Christ, the Son of God.' 'Yes, it is as you say,' Jesus replied" (Matthew 26:63–64). "The woman said, 'I know that Messiah' (called Christ) 'is coming. When he comes, he will explain everything to us.' Then Jesus declared, 'I who speak to you am he'" (John 4:25–26).

ISLAM

■ "Allah's Apostle said . . . 'If a man believes in Jesus and then believes in me, he will get a double reward'" (Hadith 4:655).

■ Allah is obligated to save His prophets from those who want to destroy them. "Then shall we save our messengers and the believers, in like manner [as of old]" (Sura 10:103). However, some of the prophets were killed wrongfully. Those who did the killing were later punished.

■ Jesus negates that He is the Son of God. "He spake: Lo! I am the slave of Allah. He hath given to me the Scripture and hath appointed me a prophet" (Sura 19:30). "Jesus . . . only a messenger of Allah. . . . Allah is only one God. . . . For it is removed from His transcendent majesty that he should have a son" (Sura 4:171).

The Exalted Prophet

The prophet Muhammad is the final and greatest prophet. Muhammad, "the seal of the prophets," is highly revered in the daily life of Muslims. At the age of forty, while meditating in Hira, a cave not far from Mecca, he heard a voice say: "Read!" He said, "I cannot read." The voice again said, "Read: In the name of thy Lord who createth, createth man from a clot. Read: And thy Lord is Most Bounteous, Who teacheth by the pen, teacheth man that which he knew not" (Sura 96:1–5).

In Hadith 1, Muhammad's preparation and role are described several times:

> Gabriel used to meet [Muhammad] every night of Ramadan to teach him the Quran. (verse 5)

> The man said, "I ask you by your Lord, and the Lord of those who were before you, has Allah sent you as an Apostle to all the mankind?" The Prophet replied, "By Allah, yes." (verse 63)

> Allah's Apostle said, "By Him in Whose Hands my life is, none of you will have faith til he loves me more than his father and his children." (verse 13)

Clearly Muhammad is at the center of Islamic faith. William M. Miller, a missionary to Iran from 1919 to 1962, wrote:

> As the name of Allah is constantly on the lips of his ser-vants, so is the name of his Apostle. As one writer has said, "One hears this name in the bazaar and in the street, in the mosque and from the minaret, sailors sing it when hoisting

their sails, coolies groan it to raise a burden, the beggar howls it to obtain alms, it is the cry of the faithful in attack, hushes babies to sleep as a cradle song, it is the pillow of the sick, the last word of the dying; it is written on the door post and in the hearts, as well as, since eternity, on the throne of God; the best name to give a child, the best to swear by for an end of all disputes." Such is the place of Muhammad in the lives of his followers around the world today.[23]

According to the Hadith, Allah will listen to Muhammad on the Day of Judgment. Hadith 2:553 declares, "Muhammad will intercede with Allah to judge amongst the people. He will proceed on until he will hold the ring of the door [of Paradise] and then Allah will exalt him to Magam Mahmud [the privilege of intercession, etc.]. And all the people of the gathering will send their praises to Allah."

Later in the Hadith comes this declaration:

Allah's Apostle said, "Allah will gather all the people on the Day of Resurrection and they will say, 'Let us request someone to intercede for us with our Lord so that He may relieve us from this place of ours.' Then they will go to Adam . . . [and say] 'please intercede for us.' Adam will reply, 'I am not fit for this undertaking. . . . Go to Abraham. . . .' They will go to him. . . . He will reply, 'I am not fit for this undertaking. . . . Go to Moses.' They will go to Moses and he will say 'I am not fit for this undertaking. . . . Go to Jesus.' They will go to him, and he will say, 'I am not fit for this undertaking, go to Muhammad as Allah has forgiven his past and future sins.' They will come to me [Muhammad] and I will ask my Lord's permission '. . . intercede and your intercession will be accepted.' . . . I will take them out of the (Hell) fire and let them enter Paradise." (Hadith 8:570)

The Prophet as Intercessor

The prophet Muhammad's role in intercession on the Day of Judgment, according to the Quran, will be limited: "And guard yourselves against a day when no soul will in aught avail another, nor will intercession be accepted from it" (Sura 2:48).

Muslims are divided on the subject of Muhammad's power to intercede on the Day of Judgment. Some say he can intercede, especially for those who have committed great sins. Other Muslims say that any kind of mediation is not permissible or recognized in Islam.

A very modern statement of the Islamic belief concerning intercession is found in *The Muslim World League Journal* of May–June 1983, where Shaikh Gamal al-Banna wrote, "Islam stresses the human character of the Prophet. . . . Therefore, any kind of mediation is not permissible or recognized in Islam. Prophets are mere messengers of God; they cannot forgive anyone if he commits a sin or exempt him from the punishment he deserves. They cannot intercede with God on anybody's behalf, for Islam does not recognize the idea of intercession as such."[24]

HOLY BOOKS

The Bible and the Quran are revered by Christians and Muslims, respectively. But there are differences in these books. (See the chart "The Bible Versus the Quran.") Muslims maintain that Allah wrote the Christian Scriptures, but human writers, such as Luke, John, and Paul, changed and corrupted them. The original Scriptures must be considered lost.

The Bible Versus the Quran

CHRISTIANITY

■ Over a period of sixteen hundred years, forty writers recorded the sixty-six books of the Bible.

■ Almost all of the Old Testament was written in Hebrew; the New Testament writers wrote in Greek.

■ All three parts of the Old Testament—the Law of Moses, the Prophets, and the Psalms—were given by God and teach about Jesus (Luke 24:44).

ISLAM

■ The Holy Scriptures, i.e., the Torah (Pentateuch), the Psalms, and the Gospels, were written by Allah and sent down to prophets.

■ The Quran was revealed in Arabic over a period of twenty-two years (A.D. 610–632).

■ One hundred four books have been given by Allah, but only four remain. These are the Tourat (Torah), revealed to Moses (Sura 2:87); Zabur (Psalms), revealed to David (Sura 4:163); Injil (Gospel), revealed to Jesus (Sura 5:46–48); and the Quran, revealed to Muhammad (Sura 47:2). Therefore, the Bible and the Quran are said to come from the same source, the same Allah.

CHRISTIANITY

■ These Scriptures were written by prophets and by apostles of Christ who were "inspired by God." They gave a true revelation of the whole counsel of God. "For prophecy never had its origin in the will of man, but men spoke from God as they were carried along by the Holy Spirit" (2 Peter 1:21).

■ By the inspiration of the Holy Spirit, every page of the Bible can speak to man and meet him in his need (2 Timothy 3:16). The final book, the Revelation to John, was written sometime in the early 90s A.D.

ISLAM

■ The Quran was brought down through the Holy Spirit (understood to be the angel Gabriel; Sura 26:193–194). The "mother of the Quran" (Ummu-L-Kitab) is in heaven, written by Allah Himself.

■ The Quran is an integral part of Allah's being. It was not created. Starting in A.D. 610 there was a telling forth of that which always was. The Quran in its present form was compiled around A.D. 646 under the direction of Uthman, the third caliph.

CHRISTIANITY

■ There are no contradictions found in the original manuscripts of the Bible (Matthew 5:17–18). Languages change, so various versions have been printed to make the Bible more readable; yet all these translations remain true to the original manuscripts.

■ Christian revelation is primarily concerned with God's coming to the help of His needy creatures, restoring a right relationship with Himself.

■ The Scriptures help Christians stay pure in a filthy environment. "How can a young man keep his way pure? By living according to your word" (Psalm 119:9).

ISLAM

■ There are twenty cases where one revelation contradicts or abrogates a previous revelation.[25] One change is the direction of prayer from Jerusalem toward the Kaaba in Mecca (Sura 2:142). Why would Allah not give this important revelation in the beginning? The reason is that "we might know him who followeth the messenger, from him who turneth of his heels" (Sura 2:143).

■ The Quran reveals a whole way of life for man's intellectual, moral, and spiritual welfare.

■ The Quran confirms the truth of previous Scriptures. "The Scripture, it is the Truth, confirming that which was [revealed] before it" (Sura 35:31).

CHRISTIANITY

■ For pilgrims, travelers on this earth, God's Word is a map to show us the way. "Your word is a lamp to my feet and a light for my path" (Psalm 119:105).

ISLAM

■ The Quran reveals clearly what the Jews and Christians hid in their Scriptures. "O people of the Scripture! Now hath our messenger come unto you, expounding unto you much of that which ye used to hide in the Scripture" (Sura 5:15).

■ The earliest extant manuscripts of the whole of the Old Testament and New Testament (the Codex Sinacticus) date from the fourth century (two hundred years before the time of Muhammad).

■ The Christian Scriptures have been corrupted and should be avoided. "A party of them used to listen to the word of Allah, then used to change it" (Sura 2:75). "Allah has told you that the people of the scriptures have changed some of Allah's books [i.e., the Torah, Psalms, and the Gospels] and distorted it and wrote something with their own hands" (Hadith 9:614).

Some Muslims claim that a gospel of Barnabas is the original Injil (Gospel) that was revealed to Jesus. Colin Chapman wrote:

> If Muslims claim that the gospel of Barnabas is the original injil which was revealed to Jesus, it is not difficult to show from internal evidence that it cannot be an authentic gospel from the first century.

- It contains historical anachronisms: e.g., the custom
  of a vassal owing his lord a portion of his cup; a no-
  tary recording a case in court; wine casks made of
  wood.
- It contains elementary errors in geography: e.g., it lo-
  cates Nazareth on the shores of the Lake of Galilee.
- It contradicts the Quran at several points: e.g., it
  claims that Jesus said that he was not the Messiah,
  whereas in the Quran Jesus is frequently called the
  Messiah; it supports the doctrine of free will.
- Certain images seem to come from Dante, the
  fourteenth-century poet: e.g., the idea of "circles of
  hell." From other internal evidence it is generally
  thought that the gospel of Barnabas was written in
  Italy in the 16th century.[26]

Muslims hold the Quran in high esteem. Indeed, they will not touch it without first being washed and purified. Furthermore, "they swear by it and consult it on all occasions. They carry it with them to war, write sentences of it on their banners, suspend it from their necks as a charm, and always place it on the highest shelf or in some place of honor in their houses."[27]

Muslims believe the miracle of the Quran proves that Muhammad is the final prophet. Shaikh Muhhammad Abduh wrote,

The matchlessness of the Quran is an actuality beyond the powers of humanity. Its eloquence remained unparalleled . . . the speaker is undoubtedly the Lord, Who knows the un-seen and the visible, and no man preaching and counseling in the ordinary way. This is the conclusion of all the evi-dences now accumulated, of contents quite impossible for merely human intelligence to sustain for so long. And thus, the great wonder of the Quran is proved. This eternal Book, untouched by change, susceptible of no alteration, demonstrates that our Prophet Muhammad is God's messenger to His creation.[28]

Muhammad is also the example and pattern of conduct for Muslims to follow. "Verily in the messenger of Allah ye have a good example" (Sura 33:21). The Hadith, which is a collection of the sayings and actions of Muhammad, show how to put the guidance of the Quran into practice. "Abdullah said, 'The best talk is Allah's Book [Quran], and the best guidance is the guidance of Muhammad'" (Hadith 8:120).

Kenneth Cragg said, "The Hadith literature has probably had as much influence as the Quran in shaping the Muslim religious consciousness. The massive authoritative collections of this material preserve accounts of the Prophet's example to the Muslim community."[29]

LIVING OUT ONE'S FAITH

The teachings of Jesus and Muhammad regarding how God (or Allah) is honored and one lives out his/her faith in the community also differ, reflecting the divergent commands in the Scriptures and differences in the nature of God (or Allah). Appropriate ethical behavior and influence on the culture are crucial in both Christianity and Islam, but the actual patterns vary markedly.

Most people living outside the United States think that America is a Christian country, and they assume most people are Christians. When they see American Christians with loose morality, such as premarital and extramarital sex, the gay lifestyle, and frequent divorce, they may think, *Who would want to convert to a religion that has such moral standards?*

ETHICS AND CULTURAL PATTERNS

We need to distinguish between Christianity and American cultural patterns. It's worth recognizing the differences between true Christian and Islamic behavior patterns, shown on the chart beginning below.

Differences in Ethics and Cultural Patterns

CHRISTIANITY	ISLAM
■ Honesty and humility are more important than preserving one's honor. "Better a poor man whose walk is blameless than a fool whose lips are perverse" (Proverbs 19:1).	■ Preserving one's reputation as a Muslim is more important than honesty. Countless young women in the Muslim world thought to have had sexual relations before marriage have been slain. Meanwhile, Muslim men who clearly were involved have not been prosecuted, and their reputations remained safe.
■ Believers should rest one day a week, generally on Sunday.	■ There is no special day of rest for Muslims. Friday is often the preferred day to go to the mosque to hear the weekly message and pray.
■ Both hidden sins and deliberate sins displease the Lord. "Forgive my hidden faults. Keep your servant also from willful sins" (Psalm 19:12–13).	■ Shame is an important societal constraint within Islam. "The Prophet said . . . 'If you do not feel ashamed, then do whatever you like'" (Hadith 4:690).

CHRISTIANITY

■ Fasting is encouraged but not required. Fasting gives Christians time to pray, teaches self-discipline, and reminds us that we can live with less.

■ A Christian is free to eat anything in moderation, but some things are best avoided. "Wine is a mocker and beer a brawler; whoever is led astray by them is not wise" (Proverbs 20:1).

■ Believers should dress modestly. (However, in the West many are often careless how they dress!) "I also want women to dress modestly, with decency and propriety" (1 Timothy 2:9).

ISLAM

■ Fasting from sunrise to sunset in the month of Ramadan is required.

■ A Muslim must never drink alcohol or eat pork. All meat must be *halal* (permitted). The animal must be butchered by having Allah's name invoked when the neck is slit. "Strong drink and games of chance and idols . . . are only an infamy of Satan's handiwork" (Sura 5:90).

■ Men should be covered with clothing from the waist to below the knee. They are forbidden to wear pure silk or gold. Women may wear both (Hadith 3:785). Modesty is required for women. For some, this means covering oneself completely when men are present. Women may display their beauty only to their husband or close relative. Most Muslim women wear a head covering. (Hair can be considered an object of sexual temptation.)

CHRISTIANITY

■ Christians should help needy people, especially fellow believers. "Share with God's people who are in need. Practice hospitality" (Romans 12:13).

■ Elders should be respected. "Honor your father and mother . . . that you may enjoy long life on the earth" (Ephesians 6:2–3).

■ Christians are not expected to name their children after anyone; they are expected to rear their children in the ways of the Lord (Proverbs 22:6).

■ Christians are to be pure in heart and to avoid a focus on their outward appearance (1 Samuel 16:7).

■ One should pray at all times. "And pray in the Spirit on all occasions with all kinds of prayers and requests" (Ephesians 6:18).

ISLAM

■ Hospitality is a very important obligation. One should be careful in turning away a visitor.

■ Great respect is shown to old people and to others older than oneself.

■ Naming oneself and one's children is important. "The Prophet said, 'Name yourselves after me'" (Hadith 8:217).

■ Muslims must wash [an ablution], remove shoes, and pray in a prescribed manner. Muslims must bathe on Fridays (Hadith 3:833).

■ Prayer is very important and is to occur at least five times daily. "When he offers his prayers, the angels keep on asking Allah's blessings and Allah's forgiveness for him" (Hadith 1:620).

CHRISTIANITY

■ Stealing can be removing someone's property without permission or borrowing it and then failing to return it. In the Old Testament, if a thief stole something, he had to confess the sin to God and return the items with interest (Leviticus 6:1–7). Christians are to resolve difficulties with other Christians personally, and deal with nonbelievers through a court of law (1 Corinthians 6:1–8). Dismembering hands is not an option.

ISLAM

■ Thieves must be punished. "The Prophet said . . . 'I would cut even the hand of Fatima [i.e., the daughter of Muhammad] if she committed a theft'" (Hadith 5:79).

PRACTICING HOSPITALITY

As noted in the chart, hospitality is an important obligation. We heard a story of a poor small village in southern Morocco that had taken in some American hippies who had come to smoke marijuana. Eventually these hippies left the village. However, upon leaving, they said that they were going home to tell their friends about this generous hospitality, and they would come back with their friends. This group of villagers actually moved to another part of Morocco, knowing they would be obligated to entertain any new guests!

The command for extended hospitality is found in the Hadith: "Allah's Apostle said, 'Whoever believes in Allah and the Last Day, should serve his guest generously. The guest's reward is: to provide him with a superior type of good for a night and a day and a guest is to be entertained with food for three days, and whatever is offered beyond that is regarded as something given in charity' " (Hadith 8:156).

ISLAMIC LAWS ABOUT
MARRIAGE, HYGIENE, ETC.

Islam is a way of living that is governed by Islamic Law. Muslims are required to live by Islamic values and requirements. Specific laws exist for marriage, personal hygiene, and even pets.

Concerning marriage, Muslims are instructed as follows:

- A Muslim woman may not marry a non-Muslim; however, a Muslim man may marry a non-Muslim wife. This insures that the children will be raised as Muslims. (In Christianity, believers are urged to marry fellow believers [2 Corinthians 6:14–16].)
- Temporary marriage (*muta*) was allowed in the early days of Islam. Shia Muslims still allow it. "If a man and a woman agree [to marry temporarily] their marriage should last for three nights . . . the Prophet said, 'the Muta marriage has been cancelled [made unlawful]' " (Hadith 7:52).
- Polygamy is acceptable. A Muslim man is permitted four wives; however, he must provide for them equally. "Marry of the women . . . two or three or four; and if ye fear that ye cannot do justice [to so many], then one" (Sura 4:3).
- Muhammad had more than four wives. According to Hadith 1:268, he had eleven wives.

Islamic Law dictates what is proper hygiene. For instance,

- The bathroom is considered unclean and the place of the devil.
- Cleaning oneself after using the toilet is always done with the left hand (Hadith 1:155).
- When answering the call of nature, one should neither face nor turn his back toward the *qibla* (direction of prayer; Hadith 1:146).
- "The prophet also forbade urinating at the place where one takes a bath" (Hadith 6:365).
- Muslims should squat when relieving themselves.

Muslim practice regarding the treatment of pets honors cats while shunning dogs.

- Dogs are regarded as unclean and should not be kept as household pets.
- Angels of mercy don't enter a house where there is a dog or pictures on the walls (Hadith 4:448).
- The thought of shaking hands with someone who has just petted a dog is repulsive.
- Muhammad had pet cats. Therefore, they are considered clean.

Muslim Attitudes Toward Western Culture

Christians and most Westerners may look at the culture of Islam, with its ceremonial washings and restrictions and multiple marriages, and regard the culture as either antiquated or superstitious. We should be aware that Muslims similarly view Western culture with caution or even disdain.

Colin Chapman wrote,

> The following are examples of the kind of general comments that Muslims (as well as people of other faiths) often make about Western culture.
>
> 1. "Your families in the West are all broken up and fragmented. You think of yourselves as individuals, and are concerned about your own happiness and fulfillment. You emphasize the nuclear family, while we think of the extended family. . . ."
> 2. "You don't show enough respect for old people. In our religion and our culture, we are taught to show respect for anyone who is older than ourselves. We can't understand, for example, how you can shut away your old people in old peoples' homes. . . ."
> 3. "We can't agree with free mixing between the sexes. We prefer Muslim girls to go to single-sex schools, and we don't allow our teenage daughters to go to discos, or at least we strongly discourage them from doing so. . . ."
> 4. "We don't like the kind of moral standards that we see on TV and in movies. We are shocked by all the sex, the violence, and the blasphemous language." This reaction is similar to the reaction of many Christians.[1]

THE STATUS OF WOMEN

Christianity has always elevated the status of women, both in marriage and society; Islam has held women as subservient and even a danger to men. The following chart shows nine distinctions between Christianity and Islam regarding a woman's role and status.

The Role and Status of Women

CHRISTIANITY	ISLAM
■ Men and women are created equal in value and ability, although distinct in certain roles.	■ Muhammad believed women have less intelligence than men, saying a woman's lower credibility is due to "the deficiency of her intelligence" (Hadith 1:301).
■ A woman's testimony is equal to that of a man.	■ A woman's testimony is worth only half that of a man. "He [Muhammad] said, 'Is not the evidence of two woman equal to the witness of one man?'" (Hadith 1:301).
■ A woman gains salvation in the same way that a man does.	■ A woman gains salvation by pleasing and obeying her husband. "The Prophet said: 'I was shown the Hell-fire and the majority of its dwellers were women who were ungrateful . . . to their husbands'" (Hadith 1:28).
■ Both men and women are sinful, but in Christ both are equally valued and regenerated.	■ Women are seen as a major cause of evil and are to be kept under control.

CHRISTIANITY

- Wives are to submit to their husbands. "Wives, submit to your husbands as to the Lord. For the husband is the head of the wife as Christ is the head of the church" (Ephesians 5:22–23). A woman submits to her husband, yet she is an equal partner, one he is to love as he would his own body (Ephesians 5:25–30).

- One husband and one wife should become one flesh.

- Divorce is forbidden in the Scriptures, except for certain conditions. "What God has joined together, let man not separate" (Mark 10:9). Jesus declared, "Anyone who divorces his wife, except for marital unfaithfulness, causes her to become an adulteress" (Matthew 5:32).

- A man's own lust is the cause of his temptation and sin. "But each one is tempted when, by his own evil desire . . ." (James 1:14).

ISLAM

- Men are in charge of women. "Men are in charge of women. . . . As for those whom ye fear rebellion . . . scourge them" (Sura 4:34).

- A man may marry four wives, whereas a woman may have one husband and thus sexual relations with only one man (Sura 4:3).

- A man may divorce his wife without reason. No privilege of a corresponding nature is reserved for the wife. However, the wife has the right to have the marriage dissolved if the husband has refused to fulfill his conjugal duty or to provide decently for her maintenance.

- The Muslim woman possesses an attraction that man can hardly resist.

CHRISTIANITY

ISLAM

■ There is no discrimination between men and women in heaven.

■ In paradise a man may have many maidens for companions (Sura 78:33). No companions are promised for the few women who reach paradise.

Whether a man or woman, any Muslim earns his/her salvation through performing religious duties (i.e., prayer, fasting, giving of alms, and pilgrimage). However, a woman can neither pray nor fast during her menses. Thus she becomes deficient in her religious duties.

Her lack of effort once each month is significant, for in Islam there is no empowering by God. Only by one's own efforts can a believer free himself from the power of sin, the efforts of Satan, and the unseen spirit world.

In her classic study, *Beyond the Veil: Male-Female Dynamics in a Modern Muslim Society,* Fatimah Mernissi concluded, "In Islam there is no belief in female inferiority. On the contrary, the whole system is based on the assumption that the woman is a powerful and dangerous being. All sexual institutions (polygamy, repudiation, sexual segregation) can be perceived as a strategy for containing her power." She quoted Al-Ghazali:

> Women must be controlled to prevent men being distracted from their social and religious duties. Society can only survive by creating the institutions which foster male dominance through sexual segregation. . . .
>
> The Muslim woman is endowed with a fatal attraction which erodes the male's will to resist her and reduces him to a passive, acquiescent role. Then he has no choice: he can

only give in to her attraction, whence her identification with fitnah, that is, chaos, disorder.[2]

WORSHIP

Christians and Muslims have very different concepts of worship based on each religion's concept of God. Prayer to a Muslim means submission to the infinite and unknowable Allah. The main purpose of worship to a Christian is to thank and praise a personal God who continues to provide salvation for His children. The purpose and approach to worship differ, as the following chart shows.

Worship in the Christian and Muslim Traditions

CHRISTIANITY	ISLAM
■ The main purpose of worship is to thank and praise God and acknowledge His surpassing worth.	■ The main purpose of worship is to acknowledge that God is master and man is slave.
■ The way of worship involves prayer, singing, studying God's message in the Scriptures, and celebrating the Lord's Supper.	■ The way of worship involves ritual prayer, fasting during Ramadan, giving alms, and pilgrimage. There is no singing of any kind in the mosque, only chanting. However, songs of the faith are quite common on the radio and television.
■ Fasting can enhance one's prayerfulness and may occur at any time.	■ Fasting honors Allah and occurs once a year, during Ramadan.

CHRISTIANITY

■ Worship should draw the believer closer to God and purify one's life.

■ Worship can be a chore if one has unconfessed sin. One's worship is acceptable if it is done sincerely, from the spirit.

ISLAM

■ Faithful worship (good deeds) wipes out sin.

■ Worship is only acceptable if the rituals are conducted precisely, with no uncleanness.

In *Islam from Within*, Cragg and Speight explain the nature of Islamic worship: "When the Quran says that God created man so he may worship Him—worship in its essential significance means not verbal praise and begging for benefits, but living in accordance with the will of God. Every right action is an act of worship. If God is truth, the pursuit of all truth is an act of submission to God and hence an act of worship."[3]

John Haines has shown graphically the different focuses of worship in his book *Good News for Muslims*, as shown on the following page.

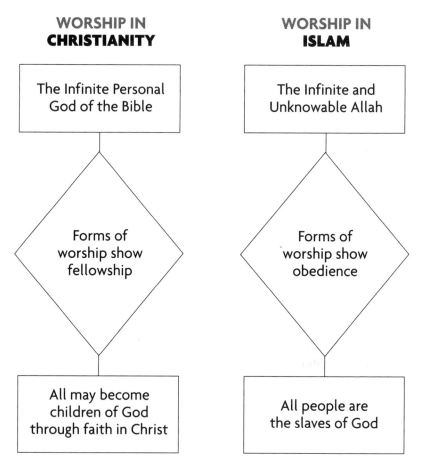

Source: John Haines, *Good News for Muslims* (Upper Darby, Pa.: Middle East Resources, 1988), 19.

THE END OF THIS AGE

Both Christianity and Islam believe a final judgment will come at the end of the age. Both religious systems expect Jesus Christ to play a major role; however, there are major differences as to how He will return and rule. (See the chart "End-Time Events.")

End-Time Events
in the Christian and Islam Traditions

CHRISTIANITY

■ Some signs of the approaching end times are false prophets and rampant sin. "Jesus answered: . . . 'Many false prophets will appear and deceive many people. Because of the increase of wickedness, the love of most will grow cold, but he who stands firm to the end will be saved'" (Matthew 24:4, 11–13).

■ Jesus Christ will return unexpectedly. "But the day of the Lord will come like a thief" (2 Peter 3:10a).

■ Jesus Christ will return to gather His children to Himself. "For the Lord himself will come . . . and the dead in Christ will rise first. After that, we who are still alive . . . will be caught up . . . to meet the Lord in the air" (1 Thessalonians 4:16–17).

ISLAM

■ The warning signs before the final judgment are: "Allah's Apostle saying . . . 'Religious knowledge will decrease (by the death of religious learned men). . . . There will be a prevalence of open illegal sexual intercourse'" (Hadith 1:81).

■ Many Muslims believe Jesus will return, live a life as a married man, die, and later be resurrected. "Peace be on me the day I was born, and the day I die, and the day I shall be raised alive! Such was Jesus" (Sura 19:33–34).

■ Jesus will restore Islam to perfection and will wipe out Judaism and Christianity. He will destroy all crosses and kill all pigs. "Allah's Apostle said, . . . son of Mary [Jesus] will shortly descend amongst you people [Muslims] as a just ruler and will break the cross and kill the pig" (Hadith 3:425).

CHRISTIANITY

■ For born-again Christians, there is no judgment for sins. (Jesus took God's judgment for man's sin when He died on the cross.) However, a believer's works will be judged. "For we must all appear before the judgment seat of Christ, that each one may receive what is due him for the things done while in the body, whether good or bad" (2 Corinthians 5:10).

■ Jesus will judge the Beast, the False Prophet, and their armies (Revelation 19:19–21). Satan will be bound for one thousand years and Jesus will rule as King (Revelation 20:1–2, 4).

■ All the nations will gather before Jesus for judgment. "When the Son of Man comes in his glory, and all the angels with him, he will sit on his throne in heavenly glory. All the nations will be gathered before him. . . . They will go away to eternal punishment, but the righteous to eternal life" (Matthew 25:31–32, 46).

ISLAM

■ Jesus will judge the people by the Law of the Quran. "Allah's Apostle said, 'How will you be when the son of Mary [i.e., Jesus] descends amongst you and he will judge people by the Law of the Quran and not by the Law of the Gospel . . .'" (Hadith 4:658). Forgiveness is based on the basis of deeds performed according to the Law and one's reliance on Allah.

■ All people will be judged on the Day of Judgment. Good deeds are weighed against bad deeds.

■ Islam believes that Allah has predestined some to paradise and some to hell. Man must by his own will "acquire" the actions Allah has predestined for him. "Unto Allah belongeth whatsoever is in the heavens and whatsoever is in the earth. He forgiveth whom He will and punishes whom He will. Allah is Forgiving, Merciful" (Sura 3:129).

CHRISTIANITY

■ Satan and other fallen angels will be cast into hell (Revelation 20:10). The earth will be destroyed.

■ There will be a new earth and heaven, in which God dwells with His people (Revelation 21:1–3). Believers will enjoy everlasting and loving fellowship with Jesus Christ. "I [Jesus] tell you the truth, he [the master] will dress himself to serve, will have them [his servants] recline at the table and will come and wait on them" (Luke 12:37).

ISLAM

■ The unbelievers will fall into hell.

■ To reach paradise, all people must cross a bridge as narrow as a thread and as sharp as a sword. The elect will cross the bridge with difficulty. Sinful Muslims may manage to cross, but it will be a painful ordeal. The time it takes to cross will be according to the number of their sins. "Allah's Apostle said, 'When the believers pass safely over [the bridge across] Hell, they will be stopped at a bridge in between Hell and Paradise. . . . When they are purified of all their sins, they will be admitted into Paradise'" (Hadith 3:620).

As one commentator noted, the return of Jesus plays an important part in some Muslim traditions, though other traditions disagree:

According to some traditions, the Mahdi (often identified with Jesus Christ) will appear just before the Last Day. He will perform the Muslim ritual prayer and go to Mecca as a pilgrim; He will restore Islam to perfection and wipe out Judaism and Christianity, destroying all crosses and killing all pigs. The Muslims will enjoy a wonderful prosperity, where the earth will yield its fruits without the need for man to do any work. Jesus will live a long life as a married man with a family, and then will be buried in the tomb of the Prophet Muhammad in Medina. However, not all Muslims would accept the validity of these traditions; none of these details appear in the Quran.[4]

DIFFERENT PERSPECTIVES ON PARADISE

Heaven, or paradise, exists for adherents of Christianity and Islam, but the concept of heaven as an abode differs significantly: Christians see heaven as a place where God and Jesus dwell; Muslims see it as a place of satisfying one's sensual needs. Muslims expect no transformation, while Christians anticipate a moral transformation that will end all sinful expression. The contrasts are highlighted in the chart "A Profile of Paradise. . . ."

A Profile of Paradise in the Christian and Islamic Scriptures

CHRISTIANITY

■ God's servants, His children, will serve Him and will reign with Him forever and ever. "The throne of God and of the Lamb will be in the city, and his servants will serve him" (Revelation 22:3). The Lord Jesus—the Lamb of God—will serve His children. "I tell you the truth, he will dress himself to serve" (Luke 12:37).

■ Paradise, or heaven, will be a place where there is no night, for the glory of the Lord lights it (Revelation 22:5).

■ Paradise is a place of no more tears, pain, or death. "He will wipe every tear from their eyes. There will be no more death or mourning or crying or pain" (Revelation 21:4).

ISLAM

■ There is no fellowship between Allah and Muslims in paradise. Allah is unlike His creation. "In Paradise . . . nothing will prevent the people staying in the Garden of Eden from seeing their Lord except a curtain of Majesty over His Face" (Hadith 6:402).

■ Paradise is depicted in the Quran and Hadith as a totally sinless place of beauty and joy. "In that day other faces will be calm, glad for their effort past . . . gushing spring . . . couches raised . . . silken carpets spread" (Sura 88:8–16).

■ The poor and humble enter. "Paradise said, what is the matter with me? Why do only the weak and the humble among the people enter me?" (Hadith 6:373). A Muslim who dies fighting for Allah, in jihad, will have a prominent place in paradise (Hadith 1:505).

CHRISTIANITY

■ The saved—those who have accepted Christ as Savior—enter paradise after death.

■ There is no marriage in heaven. "When the dead rise, they will neither marry nor be given in marriage; they will be like the angels in heaven" (Mark 12:25).

■ Those entering paradise will be fully sanctified and glorified (Revelation 21:4).

■ Believers will be rewarded according to their good works (1 Corinthians 3:11–15; Galatians 6:9).

■ In the New Jerusalem, where God shall reign, "the river of the water of life, as clear as crystal, [will flow] from the throne of God and of the Lamb down the middle of the great street of the city" (Revelation 22:1–2).

ISLAM

■ Christians and Jews are never permitted in paradise (Hadith 6:292).

■ Maidens are kept in separate corners of a pavilion of pleasure where men can visit them (Hadith 6:402). Men will have two wives (Hadith 4:468). Revelation in Islam says nothing concerning a woman having a man in paradise.

■ Those going to paradise remain as they were on earth; there is no moral transformation of their nature.

■ The saved will be assigned to different places in paradise.

■ In the garden flow rivers of water, milk, wine, and honey (Sura 47:15).

"Muslims see heaven as an entirely different concept compared with what we find in the Bible," writes Jack Budd in "Islamic Teach-In," a manual by the Red Sea Mission Team. "Christians see heaven as the place where God dwells and where we shall be with Christ, changed into His likeness." Budd notes that while the Bible describes heaven as a place "where there will be neither male or female, hunger or thirst, and where our object is the worship of a holy God, [the] Quranic picture of Paradise is" different. He quotes Sura 88:1–18: "In that day other faces will be calm, glad for their effort past, in a high garden where they hear no idle speech, wherein is a gushing spring. Wherein are couches raised and goblets set at hand and cushions ranged and silken carpets spread."

Then Budd quotes Sura 56:11–23:

These are they who will be brought nigh, in gardens of delight, a multitude of those of old and a few of those of latter time, on lined couches, reclining therein face to face. There wait on them immortal youths, with bowls and ewers and a cup from a pure spring, wherefrom they get no aching head nor any madness, and fruit that they prefer, and flesh of fowls that they desire, and there are fair ones with wide, lovely eyes, like unto hidden pearls.

Budd concludes, "The whole concept of paradise to a Muslim is sensual, and it presents a worldly picture, totally foreign to the teaching of the Bible. Without the concept of a Holy God, the Muslim relates it to a fanciful interpretation of earthy pleasures."[5]

HELL

Like heaven, hell exists in Christian and Islamic teaching. It is viewed as a place of torment, a place to avoid if possible. Christians view hell as a place of no escape. Muslims generally believe that after a measure of suffering for earthly sins, they will be released. The contrasts are shown in the chart "Different Perspectives on Hell."

Different Perspectives on Hell

CHRISTIANITY

■ Christians have varying conceptions of hell. Some say it is only symbolic; others, a place of annihilation. But many view hell as a literal place of suffering—though some shorten the time of suffering in a "purgatory."

■ Most evangelicals believe hell to be a place of eternal suffering. Jesus Christ, the Creator and sustainer of the universe, said hell is eternal. "Then they will go away to eternal punishment" (Matthew 25:46; see also Matthew 13:42; Mark 9:47–48).

ISLAM

■ Muslims believe in the ongoing suffering of unbelievers (those who do not accept Islam).

■ Hell is a state where one neither lives nor dies. "He who will be flung to the great fire wherein he will neither die nor live" (Sura 87:12–13). One will become weary from fighting against the burning fire. "Toiling, weary, scorched by burning fire" (Sura 88:3–4).

CHRISTIANITY

■ Both body and soul are cast in hell. Jesus said: "Do not be afraid of those who kill the body but cannot kill the soul. Rather, be afraid of the One who can destroy both soul and body in hell" (Matthew 10:28).

■ One must have his name written in the Book of Life to escape hell. "If anyone's name was not found written in the book of life, he was thrown into the lake of fire" (Revelation 20:15).

ISLAM

■ Hell is a place of bitter food that doesn't nourish—"No food for them save bitter thorn-fruit which doth not nourish nor release from hunger" (Sura 88:6–7)—and fire that is much more severe than that known on earth. "The Fire has 69 parts more than the ordinary [worldly] fire" (Hadith 4:487).

■ After a measure of suffering in hell, the Muslim will be re-leased. "Some people will be ruined because of their evil deeds, and some will be cut into pieces and fall in Hell, but will be saved afterwards, when Allah has finished the judgments among his slaves, and intends to take out of the fire whoever He wishes to take out from among those who used to testify that none had the right to be wor-shipped but Allah" (Hadith 8:577).

CHRISTIANITY

■ Jesus Christ holds the keys of death and hell. "I am the Living One . . . I hold the keys of death and Hades [hell]" (Revelation 1:18). Anyone "who believes [trusts] in [Him] will live, even though he dies" (John 11:25).

■ Hell was prepared for Satan and his angels. "Depart from me, you who are cursed, into the eternal fire prepared for the devil and his angels" (Matthew 25:41).

ISLAM

■ The majority of hell's occupants are women. "The Prophet said . . . 'I stood at the gate of the Fire and found that the majority of the people entering it were women'" (Hadith 8:555).

■ Hell holds perpetual punishment for suicide. "The Prophet said, 'Whoever purposely throws himself from a mountain and kills himself will be in the Fire . . . therein he will abide eternally forever" (Hadith 7:670).

HUMAN REASONING IN ISLAM

In Mark 8:31–33 Jesus "began to teach them that the Son of Man must suffer many things . . . that he must be killed and after three days rise again. . . . Peter took him aside and began to rebuke him. But when Jesus turned and looked at his disciples, he rebuked Peter. . . . 'You do not have in mind the things of God, but the things of men.'"

Jesus was saying that Peter was seeing things merely from a human point of view, not from God's viewpoint.

THEOLOGICAL BELIEFS

Regarding some basic theological beliefs, followers of Islam seem to think from the human point of view, particularly in their thinking about the Trinity, Jesus' death, the sin nature, and God's revelation.

1. *The Trinity*

Muslims believe that Christians worship three gods. They view Christians as tritheists—worshippers of God, Mary, and Jesus—whom they see as Father, Mother, and Son gods. The term "Son of God" implies to them physical procreation.

The Quran says:

> The Originator of the heavens and the earth! How can He have a child, when there is for Him no consort. (Sura 6:101)

> It befitteth not [the majesty of] Allah that He should take unto Himself a son. (Sura 19:35)

> Say: He is Allah, the One! Allah, the eternally besought of all! He begetteth not nor was begotten. And there is none comparable unto Him. (Sura 112:1-4)

Christians fully agree with Muslims that God had no son through a consort. However, as Ernest Hahn noted, it is possible to speak of the fatherhood of God and the sonship of Jesus in another sense:

> The Bible repeatedly speaks of God as Heavenly Father. God is Father in a spiritual sense. His Fatherhood does not begin with Mary and Jesus; He is eternally Heavenly Father. His name "Heavenly Father" identifies His relationship with His creatures, or what He wishes this relationship to become. . . . The Heavenly Father calls Jesus "His Son" . . . Christians of later times did not invent this title. They did not decide to turn a man and a prophet, Jesus, into a son of God or a god in the place of the living God. . . . The Son of

God does not begin with Mary. He is eternally the Son of
God. Through Mary the eternal Son of God becomes the
man Jesus.[1]

Jesus Christ entered the world in human form for a
specific purpose: to die and pay the penalty for man's sin
and rebellion. "But God demonstrates his own love for us
in this: While we were still sinners, Christ died for us"
(Romans 5:8). When John the Baptist saw Jesus, he declared, "Look, the Lamb of God, who takes away the sin
of the world!" (John 1:29).

According to the Bible, the Holy Spirit is God's Holy
Spirit. Through the power of the Holy Spirit, God's Son
became flesh, born of the Virgin Mary. The concept of a
Virgin Birth is radical to the human mind. It requires belief
in supernatural intervention. Using human thinking, Muslims struggle with this—a personal God who visits with
men and women and enters their lives. Yet the Bible reveals that after Jesus—God in the flesh—rose from the
dead, He sent the Holy Spirit to indwell believers. Today
the Spirit continues to empower followers of Christ to turn
from serving self and Satan to serving God.

The eternal God reveals Himself as Father, Son, and
Holy Spirit. Christians speak of God as Trinity, who is one
God and yet exists in three persons. Muslims misinterpret
the scriptural concept of the triune God and accept only
what their finite minds can understand about God.

2. Jesus' Death

Almost all Muslims deny that Jesus Christ died on the
cross, because Sura 4:157 says, "And because of their saying: We slew the Messiah son of Mary, Allah's messenger.

They slew him not nor crucified, but it appeared so unto them . . . they slew him not for certain."

Other Quranic references to the death and resurrection of Jesus are projected into the future. Sura 19:33–34 says "Peace on me the day I was born, and the day I die, and the day I shall be raised alive! Such was Jesus, son of Mary."

The Quran, while acknowledging Jesus Christ's virgin birth, denies His deity and preexistence. He is likened to Adam, being born by a direct creative act of God. He is a prophet of God. Therefore, He could not carry a burden for mankind (i.e., die for the sins of the world). The Quran teaches in Sura 17:15, "No laden soul can bear another's load." This is contrary to the Bible, which teaches in 1 Peter 2:24, "He himself bore our sins in his body on the tree."

Muslims say that God would not allow Jesus, His faithful prophet, to die a shameful death on the cross. They say that God is most merciful and can forgive whomever He wants. Forgiveness comes to all who have faith and good works. Sura 35:7 says, "Those who believe and do good works, theirs will be forgiveness and a great reward."

3. Man's Sinful Nature

Muslims reject the biblical teaching that sin entered the world through one man, Adam, and all men became sinners. "Therefore, just as sin entered the world through one man, and death through sin, . . . in this way death came to all men, because all sinned" (Romans 5:12).

Islam teaches that although Adam sinned and disobeyed Allah, he repented and was forgiven. People are not born sinners, but weak! The biblical teaching of the sinfulness of all men is denied in Islam.

Rather, the evil of people and society comes from

man's inherent feebleness and man's forgetfulness of God's laws. The human point of view does not like to acknowledge human weakness—let alone a depraved nature prone to sin. So in Islamic teaching, men and women have hope that by their efforts they can gain heaven. They only need to acknowledge and confront their weaknesses.

The aim of *umma*, the Muslim community, is to discipline and educate people to deal with human weakness.

Islam believes that man, by his own efforts, can free himself from the power of sin. Umma relies on individual and collective discipline through knowledge to change sinful habits.

The authors of *Muslims and Christians at the Table* suggest one place to show the futility of such an effort is to look at the fall of the first man.

> In order to help a Muslim understand how we have fallen in sin with Adam, which has affected our whole nature, it is helpful to show how God made a covenant with Adam, which he broke. Being the representative head of the human race, his broken relationship affected all his descendants. Therefore, God provided a covenant of grace for his people, by which we may be saved from our sin.[2]

The biblical solution to man's sin is found in Jesus Christ. "For if the many died by the trespass of the one man, how much more did God's grace . . . of the one man, Jesus Christ, overflow to the many!" (Romans 5:15).

4. Revelation

Muslims believe that the Quran came directly from God, that the "mother of the Quran" is in heaven, written by God Himself. They believe, therefore, that anything that claims to be Scripture but is fundamentally at odds with the Quran must be corrupt. They conclude that the Scriptures record the immoral actions done by the prophets (e.g., David with Bathsheba), give four different accounts of the life of Jesus, and include various letters written by the apostles. Muslims ask how such a variety of literature can be regarded as reliable; the Scriptures must have been corrupted and changed.

However, numerous passages in the Quran speak highly of the Scriptures. "He hath revealed unto thee [Muhammad] the Scripture with truth, confirming that which was [revealed] before it, even as He revealed the Torah and the Gospel" (Sura 3:3). "The Scripture, it is the Truth confirming which was [revealed] before it" (Sura 35:31).

Other passages in the Quran speak negatively about the Scriptures. "O people of the Scripture! Now hath Our messenger come unto you, expounding unto you much of that which ye used to hide in the Scripture, and forgiving much. Now hath come unto you light from Allah and a plain Scripture" (Sura 5:15). "A party of them used to listen to the Word of Allah, then used to change it" (Sura 2:75). In the traditions (Hadith), one verse says: "Allah has revealed to you that the people of the Scripture [Jesus and Christians] have changed with their own hands what was revealed to them" (Hadith 3:850).

Christian author Ernest Hahn wrote:

> According to the Bible there is only one Gospel, the Gospel of Jesus the Messiah. He himself is the Gospel. The four Gospel accounts in the Bible are four accounts of one and the same Gospel. . . . A multitude of ancient manuscripts of the Bible in its original languages and in translations, manu-

scripts long antedating the era of Islam, abundantly testify to the preservation and integrity of the Biblical text. There is no doubt that the ancient ecumenical Christian creeds accurately reflect the substance of the Bible in regard to the person and ministry of Jesus also: Jesus Christ, God's only Son. . . . He was crucified, died, and buried; on the third day He rose again from the dead.[3]

MOVEMENTS WITHIN ISLAM

Muhammad left no instructions as to who should be his "successor" (or caliph) after he passed away. Eventually the Muslim community divided into two parts, each of which considers itself to be the true Islam and the other a sect. The majority belong to Sunni Islam, but some 10 percent of Muslims belong to Shia Islam.

The dissension between the two—and other, smaller sects that would appear in the nineteenth and twentieth centuries—show how human interpretation has shaped and modified Islam. It stands in contrast with Christianity, whose leader chose twelve disciples to lead His church, and whose Holy Scriptures have remained consistent over the years.

Sunnis

The Sunnis accept the authority of the first four caliphs: Abu Bakr (632–34), Umar (634–44), Uthman (644–56), and Ali (656–61). They accepted the Umayyad Dynasty in Damascus to take over the caliphate. There were Sunni caliphs from the seventh century until the Abbassid caliphate in 1258. Eventually the caliphate was abolished in 1924. Sunnis are found all over the world.

Shiites

The Shiites accept the fourth caliph, Ali, but do not accept the rule of the first three. They believe that the line of successors belonged to the family of the prophet, of whom Ali, his nephew and son-in-law, was the closest male survivor. About 10 percent of the Muslims of the world belong to the Shia sect of Islam and are found mostly in Iran, Iraq, and Lebanon.

W. Montgomery Watt sums up the main difference between Shia and Sunni Islam in the following way:

> The essence of Shi'ism is belief in the imam or charismatic leader, which includes the belief that salvation, or keeping to the straight path and avoiding error, comes from following the imam, in contrast to the Sunnite belief that [salvation] comes from being a member of the charismatic community. In keeping with the essential belief, the imam came to be regarded as a source of truth or guidance for his followers.[4]

Shia itself is divided into many sects, of which the largest are Twelvers (Imami), Seveners (Ismaili), Alawi, and Druze.

The Sufi Movement

During its first century of existence, Islam held sway over a large empire in Persia, Mesopotamia, Syria, Egypt, and North Africa. Muslims enjoyed a life of luxury with concubines and slaves. Soon, however, some in the Muslim community recognized the increasing worldliness that was affecting the people in general. "They began to protest against the secularization of Islam. To highlight their concern, they took to clothing themselves in coarse cloth in the manner of Syrian Christian monks, cloth made of coarse wool called 'suf.' On that account they came to be called 'Sufis.'" They sought an experience of God and forgiveness of sin. "Knowing God personally was more important to them than anything else that Islam could offer."[5]

The Sufis appealed to verses in the Quran such as the following:

> Allah is the Light of the heavens and the earth.... Light upon light, Allah guideth unto His light whom He will. And Allah speaketh to mankind in allegories, for Allah is knower of all things. (Sura 24:35)

> We verily created a man and we know what his soul whispereth to him, and we are nearer to him than his jugular vein. (Sura 50:16)

> O ye who believe! ... Allah will bring a people whom He loveth and who love Him, humble toward believers, stern toward unbelievers, striving in the way of Allah. (Sura 5:54)

What the Sufis were looking for was primarily religious devotion and help in the problems and difficulties of daily life.

The Baha'i Movement

Three modern Islamic movements emerged during the nineteenth and twentieth centuries. The Baha'i Movement was established in 1844 by the Bab, a Persian religious teacher.

Although it came out of Islam, claiming to be a fulfill-ment of all previous religions, Baha'i is now not recogniz-ably Islam. Sacred scripture of *any* religion can be read, and prayer may be offered (three times a day) in any lan-guage.

The Ahmadiyya Movement

Ghulam Ahmad founded the Ahmadiyya Movement in India about 1889. Calling himself the Mahdi and the Mes-siah, Ahmad claimed to have received the same inspiration that former prophets had received from God. Ahmad

> said he was the Comforter [compare John 14:16–18, 26; 15:26; 16:13–15] and the "Praised One" . . . [Sura 61:6]. He also opposed the traditional Muslim belief about the end of Jesus' life on earth; he claimed that Jesus was actual-ly crucified and nailed to the cross, but did not die there! In-stead (he said) Jesus was taken down unconscious, buried alive, revived in the tomb, traveled to India, and died there at the age of 120 years.[6]

The Nation of Islam

The Nation of Islam is a recent development, a move-ment rooted in the United States in the early twentieth cen-tury among African Americans. Many identify the Nation of Islam only with Louis Farrakhan. However, the Nation of Islam movement, sometimes called the Black Muslim movement, has its roots in 1930, during the Depression that would hurt the black community even more than the white community. W. D. Fard offered a harsh, emotional message: The black people of the United States had been kidnapped and enslaved by whites. Black society had adopted the religion, Christianity, of their slave masters. Fard taught that the true religion was Islam, a religion that would empower blacks to dignity.

Fard taught that the white race was the "devil" and the black race was "divine." He urged his followers to renounce their birth names and to adopt Muslim names, like Muhammed.

Elijah Muhammed became Fard's right-hand man, and he became Fard's successor in 1934. He equated himself with the original Muhammad who had been given the Quran; Elijah Muhammed also became known as the prophet and messenger of Allah.

Members of Muhammed's Nation of Islam were forbidden to use tobacco, drink alcohol, and gamble. Strict standards of dress were enforced. Courtship and marriage outside the group was discouraged. The movement insisted upon the absolute separation of the black and white races.

"According to C. Eric Lincoln, who was for decades the leading academic authority on African-American Islam, the greatest attraction [of the Nation of Islam] had little to do with religion. Much more appealing was the idea of a group with enough solidarity and power to make a credible stand against the White race."[7]

The American Muslim Mission

Orthodox Muslims considered the Nation of Islam to be a heretical sect rather than an expression of the Islamic faith. When Elijah Muhammed died in 1974, his son Wallace D. was his designated successor. Upon taking office, Wallace Muhammed's goal was to integrate the Nation of Islam into an orthodox community of Sunni Muslims.

Under his leadership, the fast of Ramadan would still be celebrated, but according to a lunar calendar, which is eleven days shorter than the Gregorian calendar. In 1981 the group became known as the American Muslim Mission. Wallace insisted that whites be allowed to become full members of the *masjids* (mosques). The movement has grown, and his ministry claims to now oversee 1.5 million Muslims.

All schools under his control display the American flag, and students recite the Pledge of Allegiance along with morning prayers. In 1992, Wallace Muhammed became the first Muslim leader to deliver an invocation on the floor of the U. S. Senate; the next year, he represented Islam at the Inaugural Interfaith Prayer service hosted by President Bill Clinton. He has changed his name to Warith Deen Muhammed.

Back to the Nation of Islam

Not all African-American Muslims accepted Muhammed's revamping of the movement into orthodox Islam. In 1977, Louis Farrakhan announced he intended to return the Black Muslim movement to its original form as the Nation of Islam. As such, it rejected the assimilation of Caucasians into its ranks and moved away from the Orthodox community of Sunni Muslims.

Farrakhan remains known for his anti-white and anti-Jewish rhetoric. He continues to receive considerable media coverage, but the overwhelming majority of African-American Muslims do not follow him; most are members of the American Muslim Mission.

In his speeches, Farrakhan makes a sharp distinction between historic and prophetic figures. For example, the his-

torical Elijah, Jesus and Muhammad prefigured and pointed
to their prophetic fulfillment—the Honorable Elijah
Muhammed—the long-awaited "Messiah." In 1975, Louis
Farrakhan proclaimed that the late Elijah Muhammed had
risen up in him. In essence, Farrakhan not only claims to be
Elijah Muhammed's representative, he claims to be his resurrection—the second "Messiah."[8]

UNDERSTANDING CONTEMPORARY ISLAM

Contemporary Islam expresses itself in three forms:
formal, folk, and secular. This is similar to contemporary
Judaism, which has three expressions: orthodox, conserva-
tive, and reformed. Formal Islam is a comprehensive and
legalistic code of rituals and laws. Folk Islam has a more
spiritualistic, as opposed to legalistic, orientation to life.
Secular Islam has a modern, materialistic view of life. The
differences are summarized in the chart that follows.

	FORMAL (Orthodox)	FOLK	SECULAR
Worldview	Cognitive Truth-Oriented	Emotional Heartfelt	Materialistic
Approach to God	Legalistic	Mystical	Pragmatic
Primary Concerns	Ultimate Issues	Everyday Concerns	Everyday Concerns
Absolutes	Quran & Hadith	Supernatural Power	Science & Politics
Structures	Institutional	Inspirational	Social & Political
Prayer	Supplicatory	Manipulative	Agnostic & Atheist

SOURCE: Jeff Liverman, *Muslims: The Final Frontier* (workbook, Frontiers:
La Mesa, Ariz., 1977). Used by permission.

A few words about folk Islam, or popular Islam. By "folk Islam" we mean the everyday practices of Muslims all over the world. These practices seem to be inconsistent with the "purer" kinds of Islam as outlined in the previous pages. Again, we will see that Islam is driven by human understanding, fears, and superstition.

Samuel Zwemer wrote,

> The student of Islam will never understand the common people unless he knows the reasons for their curious beliefs and practices . . . all of which still blind and oppress mind and heart with constant fear of the unseen. Witchcraft, sorcery, spells, and charms are the background of the native Muslim psychology to an extent that is realized only by those who have penetrated most deeply into the lives of the people.[9]

In *Cross and Crescent,* Colin Chapman cites the following "magic practices":

- wearing an amulet (*tawiz*) as a lucky charm to ward off evil spirits;
- warding off the "evil eye" through displaying a representation of the eye on a house or car;
- writing a verse from the Quran on a piece of paper, putting the paper in water, and then drinking the water;
- using the names of God in a magical way; [and]
- drinking water from a particular spring because it is regarded as having magical powers.[10]

Fear of local religious practitioners who are able to cast curses on individuals is real. Women often are careful to discard fingernail clippings to keep them from opponents who would use them for evil purposes.

We recall the story of a young woman in Morocco, whom I'll call Sela. One day a man appeared at her parents' house, demanding one of their daughters in marriage. Failure to agree to the request would bring a curse on the family, he warned. Sela was given to this man in marriage, and eventually they had a child. This relationship ended in divorce. Some years later we visited some missionaries working in that city. This woman was working for them and witnessed that she had accepted Jesus Christ as Savior and Lord. She is now free from the fear of this curse.

In another instance a young Moroccan believer, whom I'll call Joseph, was rejected by his father. Apparently a local religious practitioner was brought in to put a curse on activity in Joseph's room. He informed me that he experienced great difficulty reading the Scriptures or writing letters while in his room. He had no such difficulty while outside his room. His father wouldn't allow me in his home.

I counseled Joseph to claim the power of the blood of Jesus Christ against these satanic attacks in his room. He later reported that God had given him the freedom to read the Scriptures in his room. Victory was won.

The influence of folk Islam is pervasive. It's like the majority of an iceberg hidden under water. The tip of this iceberg is what is visible in Islam—orthodox Islam—but below the surface is the greater mass of the iceberg, folk Islam. Popular Islam is often the driving force in the daily lives of many Muslims. (In contrast, secular Islam has much less influence, though there are many secular Muslims outside predominantly Islamic countries.)[11]

John Haines, a veteran missionary, observes: "Islam seeks to hide its inner nature. We may try to deal with our Muslim neighbor only on the formal level of orthodox Islam.

Our friend may like to be admired for Muslim belief. Yet this is often merely a dressed-up religious façade. If we are taken in by this, we will never be able to minister to the real need of our friend." The answer, he says, is to "reach within, by the Spirit from above, sent by God. . . . We must not be deceived into ignoring the reality of satanic power in the lives of our friends. They must see the truth of God's Word in its teaching about this occult world."[12]

Working for many years in the Muslim world, I eventually became convinced of the power of folk religion (i.e., sorcery, charms, witchcraft, and spells) in the lives of many Muslims. A genuine fear of the power of the unseen spirit world deeply affects their daily lives. The answer to such bondage lies in the victory of the Cross: the name and blood of Jesus Christ.

Some Muslims regard many of the practices of "folk Islam" as contrary to the teaching of the Quran, and regard these practices as compromises with paganism. Others see no fundamental differences between the formal (orthodox) and folk expressions of Islam. However, folk religion focuses on power and problem solving in a Muslim's everyday life. It is pragmatic, typical of much of human thinking today.

FIVE

PILLARS AND PRACTICES OF ISLAM

The Muslim practices his religion by observing what are called the "Pillars of Islam." These practices —performed regularly, sincerely, and correctly—will transform a Muslim's life.

THE REQUIRED DUTIES OF ISLAM

There are at least five duties, and the five reflect Islam's reliance on human thinking that one pleases the Creator by doing good deeds, such as repeating a creed and reciting a prayer again and again. Angels keep a record of one's bad and good deeds. All people will be judged on the Day of Judgment on the basis of how they kept the required duties.

1. The Profession of Faith

The Muslim faith can be summarized from Sura 4:136 in the Quran: "Believe in Allah and His messenger and the Scripture which He revealed unto His messenger, and the Scripture which He revealed aforetime. Whoso disbelieveth in Allah and His angels and His Scripture and His messengers and the Last Day, he verily hath wandered far astray."

Muhammad summarized the basic articles that a Muslim must believe: God, His angels, His books, His apostles, the last day, the decree of both good and evil.

One becomes a Muslim by repeating the Creed, or Shahada: "There is no god except Allah. Muhammad is the Messenger of Allah." The Creed must be repeated frequently, especially on conversion to Islam, on hearing the call to prayer, in the prayer itself, and at the point of death.

Real, vital faith must lead to a grid of good works, as prescribed by the Quran and Hadith.

2. Ritual Prayer (Salat)

The second pillar, ritual prayer, requires that the worshipper recite the prescribed prayers while facing the Kaaba in Mecca, Saudi Arabia. The *qibla* (direction of prayer) was changed from Jerusalem to Mecca in A.D. 624.

The prayers must be recited in Arabic. Here is the meaning of some parts of it:

> God is most great . . . holiness to Thee, O God, and praise to Thee. . . . I seek refuge with God from the cursed Satan. . . . God hears him who praises Him. . . . O God, have mercy on Muhammad and on his descendants, as Thou didst have

mercy on Abraham and his descendants. . . . O God our
Lord, give us the blessings of this life and also the blessings
of the life to come, save us from the torments of fire. . . .
The peace and mercy of God be with you.[1]

The five times of prayer are: (1) between the first light
and sunrise (*Fajr*), (2) after midday (*Zuhr*), (3) just before
sunset (*Asr*), (4) after sunset, until nightfall (*Maghrib*), and
(5) after nightfall, until midnight (*Isha*). Before each time
of prayer, a Muslim must purify himself. Pure or running
water should be used. If water is not available, the worshipper may purify himself with sand.

An imam leads the prayer. He is the religious leader of
a Muslim community or mosque. His function is merely to
say the prayer aloud, so that all may perform the actions
and repeat the words in unison. Every Friday the men of
the Muslim community (*umma*) should perform the noon
prayer and hear a sermon from the imam.

Muslims pray with their eyes open and in perfectly
straight rows. Yet a man's prayers are rendered ineffective
if dogs, donkeys, or women pass in front of him while he is
praying. "Prayer is annulled by a dog, a donkey, and a
woman [if any pass in front of the praying people]" (Hadith 1:490).

Though women participate in prayer times, they face
limitations. Women may not enter the mosque during their
menstrual period. Younger women are strongly discouraged from entering the mosque because they might care-
lessly enter in a state of impurity. Hindered from praying
in the mosque, women have a harder time having their sins
forgiven. According to Hadith 1:620, "Allah's Apostle
said, 'The reward of the prayer offered in congregation is
twenty-five times greater than that of the prayer offered in

one's house . . . if he performs ablution and does it perfectly . . . every step he takes toward the mosque, he is upgraded one degree in reward and one sin is taken off [crossed out] from his accounts [of deeds].' "

Prayers offered during the night of Qadr (the twenty-seventh day of Ramadan when the revelations began to be sent down) bring many rewards. "Allah's Apostle said, 'Whoever establishes the prayers on the night of Qadr out of sincere faith and hoping to attain Allah's rewards [not to show off] then all his past sins will be forgiven'" (Hadith 1:34).

Satan can prevent believers from hearing the morning call to prayer. A person was mentioned before the prophet, and he was told that he had kept on sleeping till morning and had not got up for prayer. "The Prophet said, 'Satan urinated in his ears'" (Hadith 2:245).

Prayer, to a Muslim, is getting oneself and one's desire in concert with the will of Allah. One accepts that which Allah has ordained for him. Fate cannot be changed. Furthermore, Islam is a total code for believers. ". . . Allah's Apostle (p.b.u.h.) [peace be unto him] saying, 'If the prayer is started do not run for it but just walk calmly and pray whatever you get, and complete whatsoever is missed'" (Hadith 2:31).

Beyond these formal prayers, informal prayer (du'a) is important. These are prayers of intercession for healing, protection, or for some special need (for example, rain).

3. Fasting

Muslims observe the fast during the whole month of Ramadan (the ninth month in the Islamic calendar). During the month, the believer is not allowed to eat, drink, smoke, or have sexual relations from the first light of dawn until darkness falls.

Every adult who is physically able must observe the fast of Ramadan. The sick, feebleminded, the elderly, pregnant and nursing mothers, and travelers are exempted from fasting. In most cases, those exempted are to make up these missed days.

> It is recommended that children ten to twelve years old be trained to fast. Fasting is one of the legalistic works that must be done in order to have one's sins forgiven. "Allah's Apostle said, 'Whoever fasts during the month of Ramadan out of sincere faith, and hoping to attain Allah's rewards, then all his past sins will be forgiven'" (Hadith 1:37). About the fasting person Allah says, "He has left his food, drink and desires for my sake. The fast is for Me. So I reward [the fasting person] for it and the reward of good deeds is multiplied ten times'" (Hadith 3:118).

Two other kinds of fasting are fasting because of a vow, to acquire merit with Allah, and fasting to make amends for a sin.

During the many Ramadan months we observed during our years in North Africa, my family and I were able to experience firsthand the activity during this month of fasting. Muslims usually consume more food during this month than at other times—because they fast during the day and feast at night. Restaurants and cafes are closed during the day and reopen at sunset and are busy until 1 or 2 A.M.

In the early hours before sunrise, "callers" move through the deserted streets calling aloud for the faithful to rise, prepare food, and eat before sunrise. For a woman who also works during the day, this can be a most ex-

hausting month. The last ten days are usually the most difficult, as everyone is tired and patience wears thin.

Many Muslims become more zealous in their faith as a
result of keeping Ramadan. Christian minorities living in
countries where Islam is the state religion often face more
persecution during this time. A close friend of mine, whom
I'll call Samuel, went to prison because an important man
in his village asked what Samuel thought were sincere
questions about Christianity and fasting. Samuel ex-
plained that he didn't have to fast because Jesus Christ
loved him and paid the penalty for his sin, so he didn't
have to earn God's favor. This man brought a charge of
apostasy against Samuel, who was sentenced to six months
in prison.

Ramadan is a time when some Muslims try to make up
for the shortcomings of the previous year. A Muslim ac-
quaintance told me that he fasted more than the required
days, hoping Allah would forgive his practice of running
around with women other than his wife.

4. *Almsgiving* (Zakat)

The paying of *zakat,* or an alms, is held to purify the
rest of a Muslims' possessions. (*Zakat* means purifica-
tion.) A Muslim is required to give 2.5 percent of his possessions to help the poor and needy. It should be paid with
the conscious belief that one's wealth and property belong
to Allah, and each person merely acts as a trustee. Another
kind of giving, "sadaga," is more like a freewill offering.

Hadith 2:545 records one honorable example of almsgiving: "I was in the mosque and saw the Prophet . . . saying, 'O woman give alms. . . . She will receive a double

reward [for that]; one for helping relatives, and the other for giving Zakat.'"

Allah withholds His blessing when one doesn't give. "The Prophet . . . said, 'Do not shut your money bag; otherwise Allah too will withhold his blessing from you. Spend [in Allah's cause] as much as you can afford'" (Hadith 2:515).

A religion that is works oriented, which rewards the giving of alms, will create large numbers of beggars. I remember standing in line one morning in a North African country, waiting to buy some donuts. A blind man was tapping his dish, looking for alms, so I gave him a few cents. Since he didn't say anything, I asked him why he didn't thank me. He said that Allah had given it to him.

The Muslim idea is that alms given are helping the giver obtain salvation, so giving is often done without compassion, and received without thanksgiving. Perhaps the giver of alms should be thankful that he can give to someone and thus help earn his salvation!

5. *Pilgrimage to Mecca* (Hajj)

Any able-bodied Muslim who can afford it must visit Mecca in Saudi Arabia once in his lifetime, completing the pilgrimage, or *hajj*, from his hometown, no matter the distance.

In Mecca, the pilgrims visit the Kaaba and must go around it three times running, four times walking. Muslims say that Adam and Eve first built the Kaaba, estimated to be fifty feet high, thirty-five-feet wide, and forty feet deep. They believe that later the shrine was restored by Abraham and Ishmael.

Near the end, pilgrims throw seven small pebbles at

stone pillars. These pillars represent the devil's temptations.

A pilgrim does his best to kiss, or at least touch, the black stone (a meteorite) in the corner of the Kaaba. He believes he obtains divine blessing by doing this. Kissing, or touching, the black stone is central to the pilgrimage experience. Muhammad did this, and for that reason it takes on special meaning for Muslims. Narrated Abis bin Rabi'a: "Umar came near the Black Stone and kissed it and said, 'No doubt, I know that you are a stone and can neither benefit anyone or harm anyone. Had I not seen Allah's Apostle kissing you I would not have kissed you!'" (Hadith 2:667).

A pilgrim is not permitted to have sexual relations with his wife during the hajj. Narrated Abu Huraira: "The Prophet (p.b.u.h.) said, 'Whoever performs Hajj for Allah's pleasure and does not have sexual relations with his wife, and does not do evil or sins then he will return [after hajj free from all sins] as if he were born anew'" (Hadith 2:596).

A male who has performed the pilgrimage is honored with the title "al-hajj." A woman is given the title "al-hajji."

At the end of the hajj, the Idul Adha (the Festival of Sacrifice) is celebrated. This celebration commemorates the willingness of Abraham's offering of his son (Ishmael, not Isaac) as a sacrifice. Allah was very pleased and provided a ram instead. Muslims all over the world join with the pilgrims in giving thanks. They sacrifice sheep, goats, cows, and camels to seek the favor of Allah. The meat of the sacrificed animal is shared with neighbors, relatives, and the poor.

According to Islam, the hajj is a spiritual journey that cleanses the soul and wipes away sins. An Egyptian civil engineer said, "This is my third time performing the hajj, yet I feel as light as a feather, as if I am newly born. . . . I wish that God would accept my pilgrimage and wash my sins away."

6. A Duty for Some: Holy War (Jihad)

Some Muslims claim holy war, or *jihad,* is the sixth duty of Muslims.

Gentle Muslims emphasize that "greater jihad" refers to a striving against sin. This is an internal battle against self and for right living that takes place in the lives of all Muslims. The "lesser jihad" is a holy war said to bear the sanction of Allah Himself. Muhammad was obsessed with the conviction that the revelations from Allah (i.e., the Quran) needed to be propagated to all peoples in the world. Jihad was important! As Hadith 1:505 explains:

> Narrated Abdullah: I asked the Prophet, "Which deed is the dearest to Allah?" He replied, "To offer prayers at their fixed times." I asked, "What is the next [in goodness]?" He replied, "To be good and dutiful to your parents." I again asked: "What is the next?" He replied, "To participate in Jihad [religious fighting] in Allah's cause."

In Hadith 2:483 we read, "Allah's Apostle said, 'I have been ordered [by Allah] to fight the people till they say: "None has the right to be worshipped but Allah," and whoever said it then he will save his life and property.'" In the Quran we read, "When the sacred months have passed, slay the idolaters wherever ye find them" (Sura 9:5). The idolaters are people who join any other god with God, that is, Christians.

Today there are Muslims who feel justified in using

violent means to achieve God's will. The Ayatollah Khomeini of Iran declared jihad concerning Salman Rushdie, who dared to write about the satanic verses in the Quran, and offered millions of dollars to anyone who would assassinate him. Almost all Muslim clerics condemned the attack against the World Trade Center in New York on September 11, 2001, done in the name of jihad by followers of Osama bin Laden. However, some clerics favored terrorist attacks against the Israelis.

There is a special enmity between the Jews and Muslims. Narrated Abu Huraira: "Allah's Apostle said, 'The Hour will not be established until you fight with the Jews, and the stone behind which a Jew will be hiding says, "O Muslim! There is a Jew hiding behind me, so kill him"'" (Hadith 4:177).

Anyone who forsakes Islam for another religion faces the possibility of death. "The statement of Allah's Apostle, 'Whoever changed his Islamic religion, then kill him'" (Hadith 9:57).

Muslims killed while waging jihad are often honored as martyrs. Also, the prophet Muhammad said that they would be guaranteed passage to paradise. Narrated Abu Huraira in Hadith 9:549:

Allah's Apostle said, "Allah guarantees to the person who carries out Jihad for His Cause and nothing compelled him to go out but the Jihad in His cause, and belief in His Words, that he will either admit him into paradise or return him with the reward or the bounty he has earned to his residence from where he went out."

When Iran and Iraq fought each other and many Muslims died, both declared jihad! Which country was on the side of Allah?

In *Islam and Terrorism,* Mark Gabriel looked at how jihad has driven Islam since Muhammad first fled to Medina:

> The Prophet Muhammad's life in Mecca [610–622] was all about prayer and meditation, so the Quranic revelations in Mecca talk about peace and cooperation with others. But in Medina [622–632], Muhammad became a military leader and invader, so the revelations in Medina talk about military power and invasion in the name of Islam [jihad]. . . . Jihad became the basic power and driving force of Islam.[2]

These later revelations that speak of jihad override, i.e., annul, the earlier revelations that speak of tolerance and peace.

MUSLIM FESTIVALS

Both Christians and Muslims observe festivals and holidays to commemorate important events in their faiths. This human nature to commemorate was sanctioned by God as early as the night before the exodus from Egypt, when the Jews observed a special meal while the angel of death spared their firstborn children during the "Passover" dinner (Exodus 12:1–14).

Yet "Islamic holidays differ in both essence and meaning from the holy days that Christians observe." As Ergun and Emir Caner point out in *Unveiling Islam,*

> First, and most important, Christian holidays remember divine intervention, while Islamic celebrations are based on human accomplishment. In Christianity, we celebrate Easter as the resurrection of our Lord Jesus and His completion of the sacrifice for our sins. In Islam, "Eid ul-Adha" celebrates

Abraham's willingness to sacrifice Ishmael, not Allah's substitution of the ram in the thicket. In Christianity we celebrate the birth of the Savior, Jesus Christ, for our redemption. Islam celebrates Mawlid al-Nabi, the birth date of Muhammad, their warrior. Christianity and Judaism recognize Passover as the work of God sparing the firstborn children of the Israelites. Muslims mark the end of their own personal sacrifice in Ramadan with "Eid ul'Fitr." The complete inversion of the purpose of holy days cannot be overstated.

Second, the communal activities and meals celebrated in Islam are exclusively for Muslims. In Christian terminology, Muslims believe emphatically in "closed communion" . . . Non-Muslims . . . are unwelcome at Muslim celebrations.[3]

Here are six special celebrations Muslim observe each year:

1. *Eid al-Adha* (Feast of Sacrifice). This feast commemorates the occasion, recorded in Sura 37:102–107, when Allah commanded Abraham to sacrifice his son and provided an animal in his son's place at the last moment. Muslims believe the son was Ishmael and not Isaac, as recorded in Genesis 22. The first day of the four-day celebration marks the end of the hajj (pilgrimage) observances in Mecca. It starts on the tenth day of the pilgrimage month (*Dhul Hijja*). Muslims all over the world sacrifice a sheep, cow, or camel to commemorate the occasion. This festival can be used as a bridge to point out the necessity for a sacrifice for our sins.

2. *Eid al-Fitr* (Festival of Fast Breaking). This is usually a three-day feast at the end of Ramadan. After the

twenty-nine or thirty days of fasting during the month of Ramadan, this is a time of merrymaking when family members visit each other. Gifts are often distributed to children during this feast.

3. *Mawlid al-Nabi* (Birthday of the Prophet). This celebration takes place on the twelfth day of the third month of the Muslim calendar. It is often the occasion for the excessive veneration of the prophet Muhammad. It generally involves an assembly where poems are recited in Arabic eulogizing the prophet, his birth, his childhood, his preaching, his suffering, and his character. Candies are prepared to share with children. This also is a time for merrymaking.

4. *Eid Rasel-Sannah* (Start of the New Year). This festival commemorates what is for Muslims the turning point of Islamic history. Muhammad "emigrated" from Mecca to Medina in September 622 to take control of the city. This event marks the beginning of the Islamic lunar year.

5. *Isra-wa-al-Mi'raj* (Night of the Journey and Ascension). This event takes place on the twenty-seventh day of the seventh month of the Muslim calendar. Muslims believe that Muhammad was taken on a winged, horse-like animal from Mecca to al-Aqsa Mosque in Jerusalem, and from there to heaven and then back to Mecca. He was welcomed by various prophets at each level of the seven heavens. This event is celebrated by special prayers and by reading the Quran.

6. *Lailat al-Qadr* (Night of Power). This is the night when Muhammad is believed to have received his first revelation of the Quran. It is celebrated on the

twenty-seventh of the fast month of Ramadan. This night is described in the five verses of Sura 97. It is celebrated by special prayers and by reading the Quran until dawn.

YOUM AL-JUMAH (DAY OF ASSEMBLY)

In addition to these six celebrations, Muslim men are required to assemble in the mosque every Friday, to hear a sermon and then pray. Women and children are welcome, but they sit at the back of the mosque or in a section by themselves. Most Muslims engage in work and business before and after the assembly.

THE BIBLICAL BASIS FOR "MAKING DISCIPLES" AMONG MUSLIMS

The call of Jesus to make disciples of all nations (Matthew 28:19–20) includes Muslims, who live in most nations of the world. Yet Christians face obstacles in presenting the gospel of Jesus to followers of Islam. One of the greatest obstacles is stereotypes that both Muslims and Christians have of each other. These can easily build barriers between Christians and Muslims, making it more difficult to reach Muslims with the gospel of Jesus Christ.

MUSLIM AND CHRISTIAN STEREOTYPES OF EACH OTHER

Listed on the next page are some stereotypes Muslims have of the West, some of which were first mentioned in chapter 3 (page 73):

1. Christians are permissive. Drugs, sex, pornography, and alcohol are widely used and practiced by Christians.
2. America is a decadent colonial power that practices economic control.
3. America is a blind supporter of Israel against her Arab Muslim neighbors.
4. Western (Christian) women are out of control, as evidenced by the way they dress.
5. Westerners don't value life, as seen in their support of abortion and euthanasia.
6. Families in the West are broken up and fragmented by divorce and children who lack respect for parents.
7. America is irreligious, as seen in the absence of public prayer.

Here are some stereotypes Christians have of Muslims:

1. All Muslims are terrorists.
2. Islam is morally bankrupt.
3. Muslims are sinister and dangerous.
4. Muslims are all Arabs.
5. Many Muslims are rich oil sheikhs.
6. Muslims cannot be reached with the Gospel.

Muslims *are* being reached with the good news of Jesus Christ. They will continue to respond to God's call until the day that the Lord Jesus returns to this earth. We must recognize and dismiss the above stereotypes of Muslims.

Christians must also believe in the sovereignty of God as they present the Gospel, recalling the apostle Paul's declaration that God uses us as part of His special plan: "God, who reconciled us to himself through Christ and gave us the ministry of reconciliation. . . . We are therefore Christ's ambassadors, as though God were making his appeal through us" (2 Corinthians 5:18, 20a).

Our God-given mission that we've been called to is founded on who Jesus Christ is, what He taught, and what He came to do. God's purpose in sending His Son, Jesus Christ, was to purchase people from the penalty and power of sin. He died on the cross for our sins. Many Muslims *will* come to believe that Jesus Christ is the Savior of the world and become part of His family. We are called to be witnesses to the truth of the Gospel. In taking this message to Muslims, we need to be firmly convinced of the sovereignty of God and that salvation is found only in Jesus Christ.

Paul wrote in Ephesians 1:11, "In him we were also chosen, having been predestined according to the plan of him who works out everything in conformity with the purpose of his will." God, not people, plays the active part in salvation. By His Holy Spirit, God does the urging. Then people decide whether or not to believe. The Lord Jesus says in John 6:44, "No one can come to me unless the Father who sent me draws him."

The Scriptures are full of claims that salvation is found only in Jesus Christ. Jesus said in John 14:6, "I am the way and the truth and the life. No one comes to the Father except through me." The apostle Peter said in Acts 4:12, "Salvation is found in no one else, for there is no other name under heaven given to men by which we must be saved."

However, God is pleased in using His people as His witnesses in sharing the Good News with those who have been blinded to the truth of God. We are witnesses that Jesus Christ has liberated us from the penalty and power of sin.

We share the Good News that the God of the universe has revealed Himself to mankind through Jesus Christ and His Word, the Scriptures.

GUIDELINES FOR CONFRONTING MUSLIMS WITH THE CLAIMS OF CHRIST

Even though a Muslim's theology differs from that of a Christian in many areas, beginning with his or her view of God as remote and impersonal and Jesus as being a mere prophet, a Christian can effectively proclaim the Gospel to a Muslim friend. We cannot overlook God's sovereign plan and the Holy Spirit's enabling power in using you and me to communicate. Here are seventeen guidelines for presenting the gospel of Jesus Christ.

1. Be constantly in prayer.

"Pray continually" (1 Thessalonians 5:17). Prayer is essential to winning Muslims to Christ. They are in the grip of Islamic teaching, which necessitates spiritual warfare.

God works as we pray. Jesus says in John 6:44, "No one can come to me unless the Father who sent me draws him." God, by the Holy Spirit, does the urging toward Jesus. He must also give faith and courage to trust only in the work of Jesus Christ for their salvation.

Pray that God will give you good opportunities to present the gospel of Jesus Christ clearly, that it will be clear to the listener, that Muslims will recognize their sin and need of a Savior and have courage to trust Him for their salvation. God has even used dreams to bring many Muslims to faith in Jesus Christ. You may pray that God reveals truth about Himself to Muslims as they sleep.

2. Be a genuine friend.

Relationships are very important. How one relates is sometimes more important than what one says! The key is one's attitude. Spending time together in various contexts will help establish warm relationships. Consider establishing a close relationship with one or two Muslims. Muslims value and will cherish friendships.

Genuine friendships take time and effort, of course. Invite your friend to your home, go on an outing, eat meals together, and help him with his problems. Immigrants don't always understand our cultural patterns. One presents oneself, not just the Gospel, to a Muslim friend.

3. Ask thought-provoking questions.

Asking questions about your friend's faith and attitudes will help you know where the person is coming from in his religious beliefs. He may be a Muslim in name only, being secularist at heart. Or he may be Muslim at heart but strongly opposed to violent acts that are sometimes carried out by Muslim fundamentalists.

Some good questions are "Do you have assurance that you will go to paradise?" or "What does the Quran say about forgiveness?" or "How do you find strength and victory against Satan?" Questions like these prove that you have an interest in spiritual things and in him (or her). By exploring the Bible together, let your Muslim friend discover the truths and answers.

4. Listen attentively.

Courtesy and respect for the other person requires that

you listen carefully. One should have a learning attitude. Respond in such a way that the person realizes that you understand what he is saying. Making eye contact is considered good manners in Arab culture. However, when one speaks to someone of the opposite gender, one minimizes eye contact.

Respect for another person's point of view is important, even if one doesn't agree with it. If we want Muslims to listen to our testimony, the first step is to listen to theirs.

5. Share your personal testimony.

As you patiently listen to a Muslim's viewpoint, you can ask for permission to share with him or her what the Lord means to you personally. Don't press ahead when your friend has lost interest. The Lord will give future opportunities.

Instead of trying to prove that God can be One and yet exist in three persons, we can share what each person of the Trinity means in our salvation, e.g., the Father, who planned to bring us into a vital relationship with Himself; the Son, who provided forgiveness for sin by dying on the cross; and the Holy Spirit, who gives us victory over the devil and helps us surrender our life to God so He can act through us.

Your personal testimony will show you that your faith is relational rather than a system of religious doctrine.

6. Use the Word of God.

Even though Muslims believe the Bible has been corrupted, they still respect the sacred books, i.e., the Law of Moses, the Psalms, the Gospels, and the Quran.

Let the Word of God speak for itself. Matthew and Luke are the best gospels to use. Read from and quote the Bible aloud. It has tremendous power to convict the hearer. The Holy Spirit will use the written word to "convict the world of guilt in regard to sin and righteousness and judgment" (John 16:8).

Read accounts of Jesus' healing and teaching. The parables give insights into the truths of God. And as you have opportunity to study together, correct any misunderstanding your Muslim friend may have of your faith.

7. Give a portion of Scripture.

If possible, give your Muslim friends a portion of Scripture, the New Testament, in their own language. Give a modern language version. Some may prefer to have a bilingual version, with English and their native language in parallel columns.

8. Proclaim Jesus Christ.

A common mistake Christians make when they present the gospel of Jesus Christ is to declare that "Jesus is God" during the beginning of a discussion. Jesus is God, yet saying so right away may create obstacles to further witness among those who have been taught "There is one God and He is Allah," and believe Christians believe in many gods. It is better to begin with a Muslim's understanding of Allah from Quranic teaching, which acknowledges God's creation (Genesis 1), Adam's sin (Genesis 3), Abraham's offering up his son (Genesis 22:1–14)—remember, Muslim Scriptures teach that Abraham offered up *Ishmael*—and Moses' deliverance from Egypt (Exodus 12:31–42). It should be noted that the Quran's account of events often varies from biblical teaching.

In many of its accounts, however, the Quran agrees with Scripture regarding Jesus' supernatural miracles, and this can be used as a point of common ground. The Quran states that Jesus healed the blind and lepers and raised the dead (Sura 5:110). One can show where in the Bible Jesus raised the dead, healed the lepers, and cast out demons (Luke 7:11–16; 17:11–19; 8:26–37). Then one can show Scriptures that describe how Jesus Himself rose from the dead, is with God in heaven, and will come again (John 20:1–8; Hebrews 1:3; 1 Thessalonians 4:13–18).

Muslims generally believe Jesus is alive in heaven with God. One could ask where Muhammad is (his bones are in Medina) and make the comparison with Jesus, who is alive in heaven. Significantly, Jesus spoke of Himself as "the way and the truth and the life," "the good shepherd," and "the bread of life" (John 14:6; 10:11; 6:35). We can mention those titles in Scripture, as well as His calling Himself our Judge and the Son of Man. In so doing, we may show that Christians are not trying to deify a man but that in Jesus Christ God became a man.

9. Give God time to work.

Be willing to allow God much time to draw Muslims to Himself through you and His Word. Muslims are often quite open to discussing spiritual matters. Some Christians think that an interest in spiritual matters means that a Muslim is responding positively to the Truth. This may not be the case! It takes time for Muslims to agree that Jesus is more than a prophet. After they make that huge shift in understanding, it may take even more time for them to believe that He died on the cross, taking the penalty for their sins.

The last crucial step is having the courage as well as the faith to trust Jesus as Savior and Lord. Islam focuses on what we must do to gain Allah's favor and mercy. The free gift of salvation by God's grace is foreign to their thinking. Be aware that when a Muslim does believe, opposition will come from family, friends, and Satan.

10. Be an example.

A consistent lifestyle of love will earn you the right to share the Truth. Building trust is critical for what you say to be accepted. In northern Africa, some Muslims would tell my family, "We have the truth, but you live as we should."

Our patterns of life can be a powerful witness. The joy of the Lord should be evident in us. Muslims lack assurance of salvation. There is obligation to worship, but little joy. Though Muslims generally believe that good Muslims will make it to paradise, they can't be sure. Even Muhammad didn't know what Allah would do with him. The Prophet said, "By Allah, though I am the Apostle of Allah, yet I do not know what Allah will do to me" (Hadith 5:266). We should be able to show others what Christianity is all about by demonstrating Jesus' presence, power, and joy in our lives.

11. Respect Muslims' customs and sensitivities.

Muslims infer honor (or dishonor) based on how they are greeted. It is essential to be polite and greet Muslims respectfully before speaking of other matters. Using the appropriate name or title for the person you're addressing is important.

In many other countries, especially where Islam is predominant, there is some distance between man and woman. Men should be friendly and warm with men but cool toward women. In most Islamic countries, one man will not ask another man how his wife is, for the second man might wonder why the first was interested in his wife! One asks about the family, and the wife is included.

Whenever possible, be aware of appropriate behavior inside and outside the home. For instance, in many countries, Muslims take off their shoes at the door. Why should the dirt from the street be brought into one's house? Allow a Muslim to remove his or her shoes in your home, and offer to remove your shoes when visiting the home of your Muslim friend.

Modesty should be observed in public. A woman should be properly clothed. Men should not show their legs. Exposing one's body in the presence of men for swimming is often not allowed for women.

Remember, we all make some cultural mistakes. A warm, loving relationship can cover all these mistakes.

12. Be informed.

Many Americans are ignorant of world geography. Morocco is not in Asia. Pakistan is not in Africa. As we get to know Muslims, we can learn a few basic facts about their country in the library. *Operation World* (Zondervan) gives excellent facts about other countries and their peoples.

It's good to know some basic facts about Muslims and their faith. Read part of the Quran. Visit a mosque; it's best to go in pairs. With a basic understanding of a Muslim friend's religious system and his or her country of origin, you can have more meaningful discussions.

You can ask such questions as:

"What's the biggest difference between our countries?"

"Tell me about your educational system."

"How does a family take care of its seniors?"

"What's the biggest surprise that you had in our country?"

13. Go slowly.

Be content to communicate one small aspect of the Gospel. Don't feel that you have to present "the whole Gospel" at one time. We must not think that one simple technique is bound to produce certain results every time.

14. Show hospitality.

Remember the injunctions of the New Testament: "Practice hospitality" (Romans 12:13); "Do not forget to entertain strangers, for by so doing some people have entertained angels without knowing it" (Hebrews 13:2).

When inviting students or immigrants to your home, be sensitive to cultural patterns. At times in our home, we have had men and women eat in separate rooms. Immigrants may feel uncomfortable eating with a fork and knife; they may prefer to eat out of a large, common dish!

Muslims should not be served pork or alcohol. Some Muslims will only eat meat that is *halal,* that was killed in the Islamic way, in the name of Allah. Explain what kind of meat is being served, and whether it is halal. If you are not comfortable purchasing halal meat, you could choose to exclude meat completely from the meal.

Muslims pray with their eyes open. Therefore, when we have Muslim guests, I usually give thanks with my eyes open. Also, it's good to explain what you are doing before you do it. One could read a short portion of the Bible after the meal. You might show the *Jesus* film on a subsequent visit.

Consider the little details that can make your first-time guest comfortable. An invited guest may not understand spoken directions for getting to your house. Send your guest a note that includes directions and your telephone number.

15. Help with practical needs.

Meeting felt needs of newly arrived Muslims can be a vital witness. I've helped men learn English, obtain a driver's license, apply for a job, and have given counsel on the job market. My wife has helped women find jobs. Also, she has taken women with their children to doctors and to schools for education helps.

16. Point out the differences between true Christianity and American cultural patterns.

All Westerners are not Christians, contrary to popular Muslim belief. Point out that committed Christians living here disagree with nude dancing, gambling, drinking, and other evils.

17. Persevere.

Continue your friendship even if your friend may not seem to be interested in Christianity. It often takes a long time for a Muslim to come to Christ. Real friendship should not be dependent on that person becoming a Christian. However, if there is no response to the Gospel after repeated attempts, you may ask God to lead you to someone who is hungry for spiritual truth. The first friendship should continue, but you may be able to make better use of your time and effort with another Muslim. Note: *Muslims and Christians at the Table,* by Bruce A. McDowell and Ahees Zaka, has an excellent section on methods for reaching Muslims (pages 173–86).

SOME CAUTIONS IN PRESENTING THE GOSPEL

Here are ten cautions in presenting the Gospel to a Muslim friend.

1. Reason, don't argue.

One cannot change an Arab's heart (or anyone else's heart) with logic. Arguing may win points in a debate, but it can lose a hearing. There are some points on which one can argue forever, yet not achieve very much, except closing a mind against you.

One suggestion in discussing various issues with Muslims: One lobs the ball back (as in a tennis match) rather than driving it back. Still, you can show passion or emotion in what you believe. Muslims may interpret a lack of emotion as a lack of conviction.

2. Don't attack Muslims' beliefs.

One shouldn't speak negatively about a Muslim's religion, his holy book (the Quran), or the prophet Muhammad.

Even nominal Muslims are emotionally tied to their religious systems, which are often observed by family members. If a Muslim asks a Christian what he thinks about Muhammad, it's best to say, "I respect Muhammad as your prophet, who led the Arab people from paganism to belief in Allah. But as a Christian, I've found peace, contentment, and eternal life in Jesus Christ."

3. Avoid some terms such as the Son of God and Trinity.

Because the Muslim will confuse "the Son of God" and "the Trinity" as a belief in three Gods, Christians should avoid these terms during early visits with Muslims. There are other terms that show Jesus' deity and unique mission. For instance, Jesus spoke of Himself as the Son of Man, the Bread of Life, the Good Shepherd, the Way, the Truth, and the Life. Also, He is referred to as the Word.

Be aware that such terms as *faith, grace,* and *salvation* may mean one thing to us and another to a Muslim. Explain what these mean to you and show Scriptures that support these teachings.

4. Use caution before inviting a Muslim to a church.

If you bring a male Muslim to church, don't seat him next to a female; men and women worship separately at the mosque. There is no singing in the mosque and no pictures on the walls. Muslims take off their shoes when they enter a mosque, and they must perform ablutions before praying.

In churches, many Christians hug each other—even men and women! Some women wear clothing with short skirts and low necklines, men and women sit together, and some Christians often put their Bible on the floor! All this may so offend your Muslim friends that they won't be able to hear the truth in church.

Explain why we pray with our eyes closed.

Before going to church together, explain the service first. Some sermons are better than others for Muslims. Ask your pastor for his topics for the next month or two; then pray about which Sunday would be the best time to bring your Muslim friend to church.

5. Avoid getting to the main point of your message too quickly.

As noted on page 133, when we "proclaim Jesus Christ," we must be wary of saying something like "Jesus is God" at the beginning of a discussion. This may throw up obstacles to further discussion. A Muslim would think that we are associating others with Allah, which is an unpardonable sin.

6. Don't spend time discussing minor points like the treatment of women or the importance of democracy.

The main difference between Islam and Christianity is not the treatment of women or of citizens; it's the uniqueness of Jesus Christ. Focus on Jesus, who gives eternal life.

7. Don't share Scripture from a Bible that has personal notes in it.

If you have your Muslim friend look with you as you read from a Bible, be sure it has clean margins. A Muslim who sees personal notes may think that you have added to the Scriptures.

8. *Men should not visit women in their home when they are alone.*

Remember that in Islamic culture, men and women do not mingle, and they sit separately for meetings and most gatherings. Therefore, a woman should not be with a man by herself and vice versa.

9. *Be careful in the use of your time.*

Immigrants need help in many areas as they adjust to living in the United States. They may be able to do something themselves or with the help of another family member. Keep in mind your goal is to help immigrants to function by themselves rather than in a codependent relationship.

10. *Look out for relational land mines.*

A man should be slow in offering to shake a woman's hand. Let her take the initiative. Because the left hand is used for personal hygiene, it should not be used in greeting.

A Christian man may call a Muslim "my friend" but not "my brother." Brotherhood assumes theological agreement.

In addition to these ten cautions, be careful in presenting information in public on Christian activities. The governments of some countries have informants who spy on others' religious activities, so be careful about giving out information on such Christian activities as church gatherings, conferences, retreats, or outreaches, especially in Muslim countries. If names of missionaries are printed in church bulletins, don't indicate the country where they serve.

HANDLING QUESTIONS ENCOUNTERED
IN DIALOGUE WITH MUSLIMS

As your friendship grows with a Muslim, you can expect questions. Here are five common ones you may receive about your faith and suggested responses to each.

1. "Why aren't you a Muslim?"

When Muslims see your interest in them and that you have taken time to learn about Islam, they ponder why anyone wouldn't want to submit to the truth of Islam!

One can say, "I respect Islam as your religion, but I have submitted my life to the will of God as revealed in Jesus Christ. Jesus alone, according to the Bible *and* the Quran, has the power to raise the dead. [Recall that Sura 5:110 acknowledges that Jesus raised the dead (with Allah's permission); see chapter 2 chart under "Jesus Christ."] All who have submitted to the Lord Jesus Christ will share in His resurrection."

2. "What about the unholy lifestyle of Christians?"

Many people call themselves Christians because they attend church, but they keep on doing ungodly and rebellious things. They have never asked Jesus to be their Savior and Lord. They lack God's help in living a godly lifestyle. A Muslim observing these self-described Christians may wonder if Christianity really makes a difference in one's lifestyle.

One can say, "To become a Christian is a personal matter. It isn't a decision of a community or nation. There may be many individual Christians living in a nation, but there is no such thing as a 'Christian Nation.' Individuals within a community make personal commitments to Jesus Christ."

3. *"What do you think of the prophet Muhammad?"*

Muslims have an unusual reverence for the prophet Muhammad, whom they consider the "seal of the prophets." Many regard him as an intercessor between God and man. Because of this adoration of Muhammad, it is unwise to make critical remarks about him, even if your criticism is supported by history.

The best answer to this question is "I respect Muhammad as your prophet who led the Arab people from paganism to belief in Allah. But as a Christian, I am a follower of the Lord Jesus Christ. He came to be the Lamb of God by dying for my sins. Now I have assurance that I'm going to heaven."

4. *"Do you believe the Quran?"*

If you have never read the Quran, it's best to say so. If you *have* read the Quran, then you can say, "I'm a follower of Jesus Christ and I believe the Bible is the Word of God. I believe the Quran in every place it agrees with the Bible."

5. *"Do not the Scriptures predict the coming of the prophet Muhammad?"*

Some Muslims will quote the word of God to Moses in Deuteronomy 18:15, "The LORD your God will raise up for you a prophet like unto me from among your own brothers. You must listen to him."

Muslims say that Muhammad is that prophet. We say that Jesus Christ was the longed-for prophet promised through Moses. The apostle Peter in his second message after Pentecost summarized the Gospel in Acts 3:18–25, referring to Jesus as the long-awaited prophet:

> "But this is how God fulfilled what He had foretold through all the prophets, saying that his Christ would suffer. . . . [He sent] the Christ, who has been appointed for you—even Jesus. . . . For Moses said, 'The Lord your God will raise up for you a prophet like me from among your own people. . . .' He said to Abraham, 'Through your offspring all peoples on earth will be blessed.'"

You may also refer to Galatians 3:16, which says, "The promises were spoken to Abraham and to his seed . . . meaning one person, who is Christ."

Clearly Deuteronomy 18:15 refers to Jesus, the Messiah who was a Jew "from among your own people." This verse doesn't refer to Muhammad because he was an Arab and a descendant of Ishmael.

DEALING WITH FOUR COMMON OBJECTIONS

As you have opportunities to present your faith in God and Jesus, you will surely encounter objections. Here are four common ones and possible responses to each.

1. "The Bible has been corrupted."

This idea of an inaccurate, corrupted Bible, not based on the original manuscripts, is common among Muslims and has its source partly in the apparent contradictions between the Quran and the Bible. Muslim scholars often quote references from books written by Christian scholars who employ textual criticism.

In response, we can ask, "Was the Bible changed before or after Muhammad?"

If the Muslim replies, "Before," he is in a dilemma because the Quran confirms and preserves the Christian Scriptures. For instance:

> We believe in Allah and that which is revealed to us ... unto Abraham ... and that which Moses and Jesus received ... and that which the Prophets received from their Lord.... We make no distinction between any of them. (Sura 2:136)

> He hath revealed unto thee [Muhammad] the Scriptures with truth, confirming that which was [revealed] before it, even as He revealed the Torah and Gospel. (Sura 3:3)

> And unto thee have we revealed the Scriptures with the truth, confirming whatever Scripture was before it. (Sura 5:48)

> And argue not with the People of the Scripture ... say: We believe in that which was revealed unto us and revealed unto you. (Sura 29:46)

The Muslim may quote another text from the Quran that has a contrary meaning. Perhaps he will see no inconsistency in this.

If the Muslim replies that the Bible was changed after Muhammad, there are many manuscripts dated prior to the life of Muhammad that confirm the Bible's authenticity. We have manuscripts from the fourth and fifth centuries. The Codex Sinaiticus from A.D. 350 is used to translate our present Gospel, the New Testament.

After addressing this issue of the Bible's reliability, challenge your Muslim friends to read the Scriptures for themselves. Blind eyes are opened to the truth through the work of the Holy Spirit when people read the Bible. If English is not your Muslim friend's native language, try to provide a New Testament in his or her mother tongue.

After confirming the Bible initially, the Quran proceeds to deny cardinal Christian truths. Therefore, Muslims must believe that the present Bible has been corrupted or they must maintain that the Quran does not confirm the Christian Scriptures. Both the Bible and the Quran cannot be truthful.

Some Muslims may be confused by the various translations of the Scriptures. Languages change, and various versions have been printed to make the Holy Bible more readable. We can point out that many versions of the Quran have been translated into English by various scholars, such as Pickthall, Yusuf Ali, Muhammad Ali, and Dawood. Each seeks to be true to the original meaning.

2. "Christians believe in three Gods."

Sura 5:116 says, "O Jesus, son of Mary! Didst thou say unto Mankind: Take me and my mother of two gods besides Allah? He saith: be glorified! It was not mine to utter that to which I had no right." The Quran's teaching about the Christian Trinity is incorrect. It tells the reader that Christians believe in God, Jesus, and Mary as three gods.

Christians should strongly affirm that we believe in God's oneness. "Hear, O Israel: The LORD our God, the LORD is one" (Deuteronomy 6:4).

Part of the problem is that Islam is a very practical and reasoned religious system. To try to understand the Trinity through human reasoning is a futile exercise. How can we possibly understand the mystery of His infinite being? We believe that there is one God and that He exists in three persons: the Father, the Son, and the Holy Spirit.

A personal testimony can be powerful. In *Understanding the Muslim Mindset*, Sam Schlorff wrote,

> Instead of trying to explain how God can be One, and yet exist in Three Persons, we should focus instead on why God revealed His triune nature to us in the first place. . . . Each Person of the Trinity has an important role to play in our salvation. It was the Father Who planned to bring us into a personal relationship with Himself; the Son Who reconciled us to God by defeating Satan, Death and Hell at the Cross; and the Holy Spirit Who indwells those who believe in Christ, in order to enable them to live for God.[1]

Attempts to explain the Trinity from nature may lead us to more confusion. Whether one uses an egg or the three forms of water to clarify the concept of the triune God, the analogy will fail at some point, causing misunderstanding.

3. *"How can you say that God has a Son?"*

Sura 4:171 says, "The Messiah, Jesus, Son of Mary, was only a messenger of Allah, and His Word which He conveyed unto Mary, and a spirit from Him. So believe in Allah and His Messengers, and say not 'three' . . . Allah is only One God. Far is it removed from His transcendent majesty that He should have a son."

In response, we can explain that the concept of sonship is seen in a special relationship, even in the Quran. The

Muslim Scriptures use the term "son of the road" for a traveler. Does this mean that the road was married and had a son? Not at all! The meaning is not a physical one. The traveler has taken on the nature of the road and thus becomes its son, so to speak. In the same way Jesus Christ, in a figurative sense, has the nature of His Father. He comes from the Father and possesses holiness, justice, and all the attributes of the Father.

The power to create life is the exclusive providence of Allah, according to Sura 22:73. Further, Allah let Jesus perform miracles, according to Sura 5:110: "Thou didst heal him who was born blind and the leper . . . and . . . didst raise the dead."

Muslims conclude that Allah is God and Jesus His blessed prophet. How would you respond?

If possible, read Matthew 9:1–8. This story demonstrates the deity of our Lord Jesus. He forgave the sins of the paralytic. Then the man was healed and walked home. Who can forgive sins, except God alone? This meant that Jesus was indeed the Son of God. He possessed God's own nature.

Focus on the character of Jesus. He Himself taught that He was the Son of God (Matthew 16:13–17). Jesus also taught in John 14:6 that He was "the way and the truth and the life. No one comes to the Father except through [Him]."

4. "Jesus did not die, as Christians claim He did."

The Muslims' denial of Jesus' death is based on Sura 4:157, which says, "The Messiah Jesus son of Mary . . . They slew him not nor crucified, but it appeared so unto them."

Traditional Muslim interpretation of this verse teaches that Allah would not allow a sinless prophet like Jesus to suffer and die. Someone else was crucified instead of Jesus, and God raised Jesus to Himself.

The Quran speaks in enigmas when dealing with Jesus' sufferings, death, and resurrection. We should encourage the Muslim to study other verses that say that Jesus did die.

> When Allah said: "O Jesus! I will take thee and raise thee to myself." (Sura 3:55; Muhammad Ali's translation of the Holy Quran)

> "Peace on me the day I was born, and the day I die, and the day I shall be raised alive! Such was Jesus, son of Mary." (Sura 19:33–34)

Explain why Jesus had to die on the cross. John the Baptist said, in John 1:29, "Look, the Lamb of God, who takes away the sin of the world!" Blood sacrifice is still a part of the ritual practice of Islam on the religious festival, the Eid al-Adha, when a Muslim buys a sheep for his family and offers it in memory of Abraham's sacrifice of his son. Just as a ram was given so that Abraham's son could live, so Jesus is God's Lamb sent to save people from their sin. We are to believe God's promise and to obey His Word.

Give a personal testimony of how you have assurance of salvation because of what Jesus did on the cross.

Read whole passages from the Gospels on Jesus' death (Matthew 16:13–21; 27:1–66) with the interested Muslim. These verses should be shared with a Muslim in an exchange of thoughts in many sessions. It will be difficult for a Muslim to absorb this truth in one sitting.

THE GREATEST DIFFERENCE: WHO JESUS IS

The greatest difference between Christianity and Islam is Islam's understanding of who Jesus Christ is and what His work on earth was. Like all major religions, Islam disagrees about the identity and purpose of Jesus of Nazareth and sees Him as less than the Son of God. Yet the Bible teaches that Jesus Christ was "Immanuel," God with us. Jesus Christ, as eternal God, became human. God revealed His nature and essence in a way that could be seen and touched (John 1:1, 14).

The Bible also teaches that Jesus Christ came as a sacrifice for man's sin, and His death satisfied God's requirement for the forgiveness of sin (Colossians 1:15–23).

In contrast, the Quran states that Jesus was only a prophet (Sura 5:72–75), and that Allah created Jesus in the likeness of Adam. The Quran says that Jesus did not die on the cross (Sura 4:157).

SIN AND A SAVIOR

The Bible teaches that man is unacceptable to a holy God because of his sin. God's solution to man's sinful condition is Jesus Christ dying for his sin (John 3:16). Salvation is freely given to everyone who accepts Jesus Christ as Savior and Lord.

Islam teaches that people are good but weak. The doctrine of the sinfulness of all men has no basis in Quranic teaching. By faith and good works, a Muslim establishes his own righteousness before Allah.

In Islam, men and women perform good deeds to make themselves acceptable to Allah. In Christianity, God makes people acceptable through Jesus' substitutionary death, which atones for their sins.

The apostle John writes in 1 John 4:2–3, "Every spirit that acknowledges that Jesus Christ has come in the flesh is from God, but every spirit that does not acknowledge Jesus is not from God. This is the spirit of the antichrist."

Islam strongly denies that Jesus Christ, as the Son of God, is God's solution to man's sinful condition. This teaching is the spirit of antichrist. While understanding this as background on Islam, a Christian should be careful about discussing the concept of the spirit of the antichrist with a Muslim friend.

Both Christianity and Islam teach that Jesus Christ will return. Muslims believe that Jesus will return and judge people by the Law of the Quran, and establish Islam as the only religion of the world (Hadith 4:658; 3:425). He will then die. Christians believe that Jesus Christ will return as King and Lord to judge the living and the dead (Revelation 20:11–15). As God, He will rule forever with all His children.

THE GOD WHO REVEALS HIMSELF

God's revelation of Himself is also a major difference between Christianity and Islam. For the Muslim, Allah does not reveal Himself. The Quran reveals the will of Allah. The Hadith, which includes the sayings and practices of Muhammad, sets the rules and rituals that must be followed to earn one's salvation. Christians believe that God revealed Himself supremely in Jesus Christ. "The Son is the radiance of God's glory and the exact representation of his being" (Hebrews 1:3). The Bible gives a true revelation of the whole counsel of God, having been inspired by the Holy Spirit. The Scriptures reveal God's plan for man's salvation, the Lord Jesus Christ.

These differences between Christianity and Islam are significant. When we compare the attributes of God as found in the Bible and the attributes of Allah as found in the Quran, it is obvious that these two are worlds apart. Abdullah Yusuf Ali lists some eighty-eight attributes of Allah in *The Meaning of the Holy Quran*. The important attributes—God is love, God is faithful, God is righteous, and God is just—are absent! Jesus Christ is not recognized as God, and the Holy Spirit is not called God.

We cannot say that the Allah of Islam is the same as the God of Christianity.

As Christians looking forward to Christ's return, we must concern ourselves with taking the good news of Jesus Christ to our Muslim friends. We are witnesses that God has liberated us from the penalty and power of sin. The Bible consistently teaches that salvation comes exclusively through Jesus Christ. He Himself says, "I am the way and the truth and the life. No one comes to the Father except through me" (John 14:6).

Jesus Christ is coming to rule as King of kings and Lord of lords. By faithfully taking the Gospel to Muslims we can hasten His coming. As the Lord Jesus said, "This gospel of the kingdom will be preached in the whole world as a testimony to all nations, and then the end will come" (Matthew 24:14).

GLOSSARY OF ISLAMIC TERMS

ablution	Ritual washing before the prescribed daily prayers.
Abu Bakr	One of Muhammad's closest followers, who was the successor of Muhammad from A.D. 632–634.
adhan	The call to prayer made five times a day.
ahl al-dhimmi	Literally, "people of protection." A special status given by Muslims to people of the covenant (i.e., Christians and Jews) which allowed these groups to have a second-class status

and retain their places and customs of worship.

Ahl al-Kitab   "People of the Book," a term in the Quran that designates Christians and Jews in the Quran.

Al-Fatiha   "The opening"; the name of the first sura of the Quran. It is repeated several times during each of the five times of prayer each day.

al-hajj   A Muslim who has made the pilgrimage (hajj) to Mecca.

al-janna   "The garden," the Muslim name for paradise, which will be the abode of the Muslims for eternity.

Allah's Apostle   An honorific title for Muhammad.

Allahu Akbar   "Allah is the Most Great," repeated as part of a Muslim's prayers.

ansar   "Helpers," specifically, companions and supporters of Muhammad in Medina.

asr   The third, or afternoon, prayer.

ayat   Verse of the Quran.

ayatollah	"The eye of Allah," a term designating the chief religious leaders of the Shiite Muslims.
baraka	A blessing.
caliph	An Islamic ruler who was a close associate of Muhammad or the descendant of one. He was the representative of both Allah and Muhammad.
caliphate	The Muslim state headed by a caliph; the last one ended with the collapse of the Ottoman Empire in 1924.
dar al-harb	"Abode of War" or "house of war," a designation given to all people who resist submitting to the will of Allah.
dar al-Islam	"Abode of Islam" is a designation given to Muslims who have submitted to the will of Allah.
da'wah	"An invitation," calling all people to the path of Allah; the Arabic term for missionary work.
day of resurrection	The last day, when all men will be resurrected and judged by Allah.

din

Religion in general and religious duties in particular, including the five duties of Islam.

Eid al-Adha

The celebration which closes the season of hajj (pilgrimage). Sheep, cows, and camels are sacrificed in memory of Abraham's offering his son Ishmael as a sacrifice to Allah and Allah's providing a ram instead.

Eid al-Fitr

Feast of the breaking of the fast of Ramadan.

fajr

The first prayer at dawn.

Fatima

The best known of the daughters of Muhammad.

fatwa

Legal ruling made by an expert scholar.

Gabriel

The angel through whom Allah revealed the Quran to Muhammad from A.D. 610–623.

Hadith

The collection of traditions regarding the life and sayings of the prophet Muhammad and how he responded to others. These traditions were first transmitted by word of mouth and later recorded. The second source for the Shari´a.

hafiz	Title of respect given to one who has memorized the total Quran.
hajj	"Pilgrimage," specifically the pilgrimage made to Mecca once in a person's lifetime. This is one of the five required duties of Islam.
halal	"Permitted"; meat that is properly butchered in the name of Allah, with its head facing Mecca.
haram	"Unlawful"; doing that which is forbidden according to Islam.
hell (fire)	The place of torment, said to have seven divisions or portals (Sura 15:44). Often referred to as an-Nar ("the fire") in the Quran.

1. Jahannam, the purgatorial hell for Muslims.
2. Laza, a blazing fire for Christians.
3. Al-Hutamah, an intense fire for the Jews.
4. Sair, a flaming fire for Sabians.
5. Saqar, a scorching fire for the Magi.
6. Al-Jahim, a huge, hot fire for idolaters.
7. Hawiyah, bottomless pit for the hypocrites. [1]

Hezbollah	"The Party of God,"; the political/ religious group associated with the late Ayatollah Khomeini. This group is influential among Lebanese Shiites.
hijab	Scarf worn by Muslim women over their head.
Hijira	In A.D. 622, Muhammad fled to Medina from Mecca. This is the beginning date of the Muslim lunar calendar.
Hira Cave	A mountain near Mecca where Muhammad received the first revelations of the Quran.
ijma	General consensus of the community and the ulama; the third source of Islamic law.
imam	The person who leads the ritual law; the religious leader of the Muslim community; plural is ulama.
Injil	Arabic word for "the Gospels," by which is meant the Christian New Testament.
Inshallah	"If God wills"; often said in hopes that God will bring something desired to pass.

Islam	Submitting to the will of Allah; to make peace by laying down one's arms in submission.
jihad	Striving in the path of Allah; "greater jihad" refers to the spiritual warfare against sin; "lesser jihad" is fighting for the cause of Allah and bringing all human beings into submission to Allah.
jinn	Spirit beings; jinn can be good or bad.
jizya	"Tax"; a tax imposed upon all non-Muslims who are living in and under protection of the Muslim government.
Kaaba	The cube-shaped building in the center of the mosque in Mecca, with the black meteorite in the corner. This is the chief destination for the Muslim pilgrimage.
kafir	"Unbeliever" or infidel; one who refuses to believe and submit to Allah.
Khadija	The first wife of Muhammad.
marabout	A North African Muslim leader endowed with baraka (blessing).

masjid — The Arabic word that means "mosque"; it is also the designation by African-American Muslims for their places of worship (i.e., a Masjid Muhammad).

Mecca — Holy city in Saudi Arabia; where Muhammad began his ministry.

Medina — The second most holy city to Muslims; the city to which Muhammad fled upon leaving Mecca in A.D. 622.

mosque — The Muslim place of worship.

muazzin — One who gives the call to prayer.

mujahideen — Men who fight in the cause of Allah.

Muslim — One who submits to the will of Allah.

muta — Temporary marriage; still practiced by Shiites.

paradise — Place of eternal reward for all faithful Muslims.

qadi — "Judge" who serves in both Islamic and civil court.

qibla — Niche in a wall of the mosque noting the direction of Mecca, toward the Kaaba, toward which all Muslims must pray.

qiyas	"An analogical reasoning"; the fourth source for the Shari´a.
Quran	The Holy book revealed by the angel Gabriel to Muhammad; the first source for the Shari´a.
rak'at	The prayers of Muslims, consisting of one standing, one bowing, and two prostrated.
Ramadan	The month of fasting; the ninth month of the Muslim calendar.
rasul	"Apostle"; "messenger"; a prophet who is distinguished by having brought both a message and scripture from Allah. Moses, David, Jesus, and Muhammad all bear the title of rasul.
salat	The liturgical form of prayer five times a day; the second of the five duties of Islam.
Shahada	"The witness," the creed of all Muslims: "There is no God but Allah, and Muhammad is his messenger." Making this confession before two witnesses makes one a Muslim; first of the five duties of Islam.

Shari´a   "The path." The divine will for all Muslims applied to every situation in life. It is derived from the Quran, the Hadith, general consensus, and qiyas (analogy).

sheikh   "Old man"; a Muslim scholar who is often elevated to leadership because of his great learning.

Shia   The branch of Islam who believe that the successors of Muhammad should have been limited to his own personal family. Thus Ali, Muhammad's cousin and designated heir, should have been the first caliph. Most people in Iran and many Muslims in Iraq and Lebanon are Shia.

shirk   Associating partners to Allah (i.e., saying that Jesus Christ is the Son of God); the unforgivable sin.

Sufi   A Muslim who has a mystical approach to Islam, seeking direct knowledge and experience of Allah.

sunnah   The practices and way of life of Muhammad. This is a model to be followed. It is the way of faith and conduct as followed by the Muslim community.

Sunni	One of the two large branches of Islam. Sunnis make up approximately 90 percent of all Muslims. They believe that the successors of Muhammad should have been chosen from among Muhammad's followers, not limited to Muhammad's personal family.
sura	A chapter of the Quran; there are 114 of them.
tahrif	The doctrine that teaches that the Jews and Christians have corrupted the Scriptures.
talaq	Divorce by repudiation; the husband merely repeats the words "I divorce you" three times.
Tawhid	The oneness of Allah; He is unitary, without persons. Devout believers worship this superdimensional God, living before Him in fear and reverence, observing all His laws in obedience.
Tourat	"The Torah" (Pentateuch).
ulama	Plural of imam; spiritual leaders of the Muslim community and custodians of Islamic teachings.

umma   The worldwide community of Muslims. It has a common adherence to a sacred culture based on the Quran, which makes it a tenacious community. There is little liberty for the born Muslim to move out of this community.

wudu   "Ablution" (ceremonial cleansing) performed before prayers.

Yathrib   The name of the city of Medina before the arrival of Muhammad in A.D. 622.

Yesua   Arabic name for Jesus from the Hebrew root; *Isa* is the Quranic name for Jesus.

zabur   "The Psalms" revealed to the prophet David.

zakat   Almsgiving; the 2.5 percent offering given for the cause of Islam; the third of the five duties (pillars) of Islam.

zuhr   The second (noon) prayer.

RESOURCE LIST

UNDERSTANDING ISLAM

Chapman, Colin. *Cross and Crescent: Responding to the Challenge.* Downers Grove, Illinois: InterVarsity, 1995.

Cragg, Kenneth, and Speight, R. Marston. *Islam from Within: Anthology of a Religion.* Belmont, California: Wadsworth Publishing, 1980.

Parshall, Phil. *Inside the Community.* Grand Rapids, Michigan: Baker, 1994.

_____. *The Cross and the Crescent: Understanding the Muslim Mind and Heart.* Wheaton, Illinois: Tyndale, 1989.

Poston, Larry A., and Ellis, Carl F., Jr. *The Changing Face of Islam in America.* Camp Hill, Pennsylvania: Horizon, 2000.

Schlorff, Sam. *Understanding the Muslim Mindset.* Upper Darby, Pennsylvania: Arab World Ministries, Inc. 1995.

Shorrosh, Anis A. *Islam Revealed: A Christian Arab's View of Islam.* Nashville,: Thomas Nelson, 1988.

Watt, W. Montgomery. *Bell's Introduction to the Quran.* Edinburgh: Edinburgh University Press, 1970.

Zwemer, Samuel M. *The Muslim Christ.* Edinburgh: Oliphant, Anderson, and Ferrier, 1912.

_____. *The Moslem Doctrine of God.* 1905; Reprint. Gerrads Cross, Great Britain: WEC, 1981.

WITNESS AMONG MUSLIMS

Abdul-Haqq, Abdiyah Akbar. *Sharing Your Faith with a Muslim.* Minneapolis, Minnesota: Bethany Fellowship, Inc., 1980.

Campbell, William. *The Quran and the Bible in the Light of History and Science.* Upper Darby, Pennsylvania: Middle East Resources, n.d.

Haines, John. *Good News for Muslims.* Upper Darby, Pennsylvania: Middle East Resources, 1998.

Livingstone, Greg. *Planting Churches in Muslim Cities.* Grand Rapids, Michigan: Baker, 1993.

Love, Rick. *Muslims, Magic, and the Kingdom of God.* Pasadena, California: William Carey Library, 2000.

McDowell, Bruce A., and Zaka, Anees. *Muslims and Christians at the Table.* Phillipsburg, New Jersey: Presbyterian & Reformed Publishing, 1999.

Musk, Bill A. *The Unseen Face of Islam: Sharing the Gospel with Ordinary Muslims.* East Sussex: MARC Evangelical Missionary Alliance, 1989.

Parshall, Phil. *Bridge to Islam: A Christian's Perspective on Folk Islam.* Grand Rapids, Michigan: Baker, 1983.

Saal, William. *Reaching Muslims for Christ.* Chicago, Illinois: Moody Press, 1993.

Schlorff, Sam. *Discipleship in Islamic Society.* Marseilles, France: Ecole Radio Biblique, 1981.

Woodberry, J. Dudley, ed. *Muslims and Christians on the Emmaus Road.* Monrovia, California: MARC, 1989.

NOTES

Preface

1. Timothy George, *Is the Father of Jesus the God of Islam?* (Grand Rapids: Zondervan, 2002), 25.

Chapter 1: Is True Islam Peaceful or Militant?

1. Mark A. Gabriel, *Islam and Terrorism* (Lake Mary, Fla.: Charisma House, 2002), 69–70.

2. Cited in Rev. Canon Sell, *The Historical Development of the Quran* (Oak Park, Ill.: People International, n. d.), 1–2.

3. Cited in Phil Parshall, *Inside the Community* (Grand Rapids: Baker, 1994), 12.

4. Ergun Mehmet Caner and Emir Fethi Caner, *Unveiling Islam* (Grand Rapids: Kregel, 2002), 96.

Chapter 2: Significant Differences Between Christianity and Islam

1. Cited in Jack Budd, "Islamic 'Teach In'" (manual, Red Sea Mission Team, London, n. d.), 29.

2. Ibid., 16.

3. Samuel M. Zwemer, *The Moslem Doctrine of God* (New York: American Tract Society, 1905), 49.

4. In this side-by-side chart, "Unity and Trinity," the words *God* and *Allah* are used synonymously. (Muslims consider Allah to be God.) Note, however, that the God of the Bible and Allah of the Quran don't have the same character and attributes.

5. Zwemer, *The Moslem Doctrine of God*, 76.

6. Ibid.

7. Colin Chapman, *Cross and Crescent* (Downers Grove, Ill.: Inter-Varsity, 1995), 10.

8. Cited in Zwemer, T*he Moslem Doctrine of God*, 84.

9. Isma'il Ragi al-Faruqi, *Christian Ethics* (Montreal: McGill Univ. Press, 1967), 225.

10. Bruce A. McDowell and Anees Zaka, *Muslims and Christians at the Table* (Phillipsburg, N. J.: P&R Publishing, 1999), 109.

11. Ibid., 94.

12. Budd, "Islamic 'Teach In,'" 28.

13. McDowell and Zaka, *Muslims and Christians*, 100–101.

14. Sam Schlorff, *Understanding the Muslim Mindset* (Upper Darby, Pa.: Arab World Ministries, 1995), 5.

15. McDowell and Zaka, *Muslims and Christians*, 90.

16. Schlorff, *Understanding the Muslim Mindset*, 3.

17. Zwemer, *The Moslem Doctrine of God*, 67–68.

18. McDowell and Zaka, *Muslims and Christians*, 104–05.

19. Ibid., 150.

20. Ibid., 131.

21. Timothy George, *Is the Father of Jesus the God of Islam?* (Grand Rapids: Zondervan, 2002), 115–16.

22. McDowell and Zaka, *Muslims and Christians*, 123–24.

23. William M. Miller, *A Christian Response to Islam* (Phillipsburg, N. J.: Presbyterian & Reformed, 1976), 51.

24. Shaikh Gamal al-Banna, "The Islamic Concept of God and Prophet," *The Muslim World League Journal* May–June 1983; as cited in William Campbell, *The Quran and the Bible in the Light of History and Science* (Upper Darby, Pa.: Middle East Resources, n. d.), 295.

25. Thomas Patrick Hughes, *Hughes' Dictionary of Islam* (Chicago: Kazi, 1995), 520.

26. Chapman, *Cross and Crescent*, 189.

27. Anis A. Shorrosh, *Islam Revealed* (Nashville: Nelson, 1988), 19.

28. Shaikh Muhammad Abduh, *The Theology of Unity* (London: George & Allen, 1965), as quoted in Kenneth Cragg and R. Marston Speight, *Islam from Within* (Belmont, Calif.: Wadsworth, 1980), 20.

29. Cragg and Speight, *Islam from Within*, 78.

Chapter 3: Living Out One's Faith

1. Colin Chapman, *Cross and Crescent* (Downers Grove, Ill.: Inter-Varsity, 1995), 29–30.

2. Quoted in Fatimah Mernissi, *Beyond the Veil* (Cambridge, Mass.: Schenkman, 1975), as cited in Kenneth Cragg, R. Marston Speight, *Islam from Within* (Belmont, Calif.: Wadsworth, 1980), 240–41.

3. Ibid., 39.

4. ABD-UL-MASIH, *Islam and Christianity* (Ibadan, Nigeria: Daystar, 1965), 15.

5. Jack Budd, "Islamic 'Teach In'" (manual, Red Sea Mission Team, London, n.d.), 33–34.

Chapter 4: Human Reasoning in Islam

1. Ernest Hahn, *Understanding Some Muslim Misunderstanding* (Toronto: Fellowship of Faith, n.d.), 4.

2. Bruce A. McDowell and Anees Zaka, *Muslims and Christians at the Table* (Phillipsburg, N. J.: P&R Publishing, 1999), 126.

3. Ernest Hahn, *Muslim Misunderstandings*, 11.

4. W. Montgomery Watt, *The Muslim Intellectual: A Study of al-Ghazali* (Edinburgh: Edinburgh Univ. Press, 1963), 80.

5. Abdiyah Akbar Abdul-Haqq, *Sharing Your Faith with a Muslim* (Minneapolis: Bethany, 1980), 168–69.

6. ABD-UL-MASIH, *Islam and Christianity* (Ibadan, Nigeria: Daystar, 1965), 34.

7. Larry A. Poston with Carl F. Ellis Jr., *The Changing Face of Islam in America* (Camp Hill, Pa.: Horizon, 2000), 114.

8. Ibid., 158.

9. As quoted in Don M. McCurry, *The Gospel and Islam* (Monrovia, Calif.: MARC, 1978), 209.

10. Colin Chapman, *Cross and Crescent* (Downers Grove, Ill.: Inter-Varsity, 1995), 122.

11. Secular Muslims follow Islam in varying degrees. They may pray, they may fast, but they are not committed to the faith. Those embracing secular Islam do not practice all five pillars of the faith (described in chapter 5).

12. John Haines, *Good News for Muslims* (Upper Darby, Pa.: Middle East Resources, 1988), 99–100.

Chapter 5: Pillars and Practices of Islam

1. ABD-UL-MASIH, *Islam and Christianity* (Ibadan, Nigeria: Daystar, 1965), 22.

2. Mark A. Gabriel, *Islam and Terrorism* (Lake Mary, Fla: Charisma House, 2002), 31.

3. Ergun Mehmet Caner and Emir Fethi Caner, *Unveiling Islam* (Grand Rapids: Kregel, 2002), 159.

Chapter 6: The Biblical Basis for "Making Disciples" Among Muslims

1. Sam Schlorff, *Understanding the Muslim Mindset* (Upper Darby, Pa.: Arab World Ministries, 1995), 17.

Glossary

1. Thomas Patrick Hughes, *Dictionary of Islam* (Chicago: Kazi, 1995), 171; as quoted in Phil Parshall, *Inside the Community* (Grand Rapids: Baker, 1994), 226.

The author, Dave Goldmann, conducts a seminar on
"Understanding and Reaching Muslims."
The seminar increases one's confidence, skill, and comfort
in relating to North American Muslims.

Churches and groups can reach Dave at:
www.goldmannseminars.org

ISLAM AND THE BIBLE TEAM

ACQUIRING EDITOR
Mark Tobey

COPY EDITOR
Jim Vincent

BACK COVER COPY
Anne Perdicaris

COVER DESIGN
Ragont Design

INTERIOR DESIGN
Ragont Design

PRINTING AND BINDING
Bethany Press International

The typeface for the text of this book is
Sabon